HEATHER

YOU ARE BREATHTAKING
AS A HUMAN BEING MY
FRIEND. THANK YOU FOR
FRIENDSHIP, SUPPORT,
AND CONVERSATION

Shannon
D.
Hughes

Movement Mastery

How to Find Your Motivation and Create Lasting Momentum

Shannon Hughes

Speaker House Publishing

Movement Mastery: How to Find Your Motivation and Create Lasting Momentum

Sdhughesenterprises@gmail.com

Published by Speaker House Publishing

ISBN 978-1-7328235-7-0

Cover and back design by Michael de Hoyos, Jr.

Printed in the United States of America.

Table of Contents

Dedication

To my mother and father Charles and Earlene. To my twin brother Terrence and my niece Selena. To both of my Grandmothers, and the Hughes, Smith, Johnson and Martin Family.

Special Thanks

To Dr. Dorothy Bounds, Earl Bounds and the rest of the Dorolyn Academy of Music family. To the 20 years of teaching music, the best years of my life. To Donald "Buster" Woods and my brother, I thank you.

To Chris Terry, Dexter Sims, Audra Wilson, Aida Brenston, Robert "Bobby" Washington, Brian Pettis, Doreen Hall, John Henderson, Ravey Barren, and Shayla Lamar and the Lamar family. I couldn't have gotten better as a music teacher and person without you all.

I thank all of my music students as well. I grew because of you.

To Alli T. Covington and the BOD Company. To my good friend and co-host at "Good Day Orange County," Lauren Solomon. To Janet Rodriguez, founder of AAB "All Access Broadcasting" in Beverly Hills. To the "Shake It Up Now" founder and talk show host at AAB, Julie Sands. To my friend Scott DeMoulin and his lovely wife Dallyce. To founder of Voice America, Jeff Spenard. To everyone at Voice America including Ryan Treasure. To Tracy Trump, founder of The

Speakers Coalition. To Allison H. Larsen, speaker, author and host of her own show on Voice America. Allison H. Larsen thank you so much. To billionaire business strategist Forbes Riley. I thank you.

To ICON Founder and former CEO of Guerrilla Marketing, David T. Fagan and his team. I couldn't have done this without you. To Abigail Gazda, founder of Hearts Unleashed. Thank you for your vision and guidance. To Kimberly Hardin-Thorpe, owner of Treasure Coast Sotheby's International Realty in Florida. THANK YOU. To a complete stranger who decided to help me for whatever reason. Kimberly my eternal thanks.

To the phenomenal Chris Salem, I thank you sir. To Bryant Hunt, Carlee "CK" Koehler, and Kent Clothier. To the REWW Team. To Chris Buttrum, Jeff Henry, Rebecca Jensen, Sammi Tucker, Zaundra Grant, and Alysa Rushton.

To Keutmany "Blue Ivy" Chansilaphet a.k.a. DJ KiKi. Please support her music on iTunes. She is the number #1 DJ in Las Vegas and one of the top 100 DJanes in the world.

To Mahsheed Barghisavar, Jackie Marquez, Adriana Jaime, Oscar Perez, Simone Jackson, Josephine Sherman, Nieca Hickland, Russ Dixon, George, Mia, Natalia, Giselle, Zoe and Mama B. To Jennifer Schumacher, Jay, and Vickie and Olivia Adams.

To my BFF Latoya "Ice Princess" Taylor and her son and my Godson, Marlon. I love you both. To Lora "LL" Luna, and Angelica Vaimaona. To my two favorite Kelseys in the world, Viehmann and Olivero. You two are DYNAMITE!! To the Unstoppable and successful Business Coach Kelly Roach. I owe you so much.

To my new EZ Way family and founder Eric Zuley. Thanks for putting me on the EZ Way Hall of Fame. To Jennifer "crazy like a fox" Fox, Jeannine Orozco, Brandon Gyles, Carl Williams, Donovan "Nutzo" Oliver, Janelle "Nelly Curl" Dobyne, and Elisha Teague. To Lora Polowczuk. You are a Superstar. To Shawn Jones and Rosemary Sambora. To Kari Warberg Block, Laura J. Hamilton, Frank Saltzburg, Christina "Nina Ross" Penson, Tony Gaskins, Loukia Mastrodimos, and Jenny Sepulveda. To the founder of Along Comes Hope for Cancer, Jenny Mulks. To Jake Muellner, Matt Mesick, and Julia "my Toronto girl" Sapershteyn. I have MAD RESPECT for you.

To Gail Scott, Jerome "JP" Pearce, Sandy Cesaire, Robert Syfert, Matthew and Orna Walters, Craig and Jenny Dumnich, Wylene Benson, and Holly Porter. To CEO founder and long-time friend Andria Stennis-Hudson. To Donna Guinourard, Jeremy Rohrbach and family. To the John Maxwell Team. To my extended family at Yoga by Degrees. To CEO of Minerva Enterprises and award-winning TV host of e360, Cindy Ashton. To Beth and Jeff Johnson and Vashti Beharry. To probably my greatest fan, Yamili Saucedo. I thank you.

To Sheelah White. I thank you from the bottom of my heart. To Dan Tyler. Your friendship is one of the best things in my life. To Gina Pegg, Julie May, my little sis Autum Newsome, and Teresa "tough as nails" Snider.

To International Speaker and fellow John Maxwell team member and friend, Annica Torneryd. To Michael and Michelle Rohaley, Isabel Donadio, Robin O'Reilly, Genesia Elizabeth, Gilbert Dean Arcillas, Linda Ann Harms, and Grace Jo. I cannot give you enough thanks.

To the host of The Rico No Suave Show in Chicago, Rico Mangram. To C. Douglas Conlan, Kasia Weszczak, Carolyn Webber, Derek and Jules and my extended family at iLoveKickboxing in LaGrange Park Illinois. To Misty Boring and Tony S. DUrso. Thank you for helping me launch my internet show. To Samantha Iacobelli. To Antoine Jack my longtime barber and brother. To Lisa Williams one of the strongest people I know. No health issue will beat you. You are the ULTIMATE SURVIVOR.

To Dannella Burnett, and Antoinette "Lovely Lyricist" Coleman. To Les Brown. Les, thank you for my one time meeting you in Las Vegas in July 2017. To Pastors Linda and Curtis Stennis, Pastor DeAndre Patterson and his lovely wife Pat. To Frances Bueno Khawly. To Kimberly Johnson. You are an absolutely BEAUTIFUL SOUL. To Miranda Booker. To Cancer Champion and Creator of Service Heros, Tamara Hunter. To Chris Wise, Livia Caudell, Denisha Tate-McAlister, Darrell E. Garrison, Euri Jimenez, Karen Rose, Andy Shiparski, Bill Stillwell, Erica Lawrence, Tony, Roselle and Logan Acierto. To Elise Larsen, Kelia Guyton, and Adria Yvonne (RIP my high school friend). To the Calloway Family, especially to Valerie. To the former Anchor Reporter at KWCH 12 Eyewitness News, Angela Monroe. To Cecile, Camara and the rest of the Brown family. To my cousin and radio personality, Alexx Dupri. To Zoe Munoz, Phyllis Polvi and family. And finally, to Leon, Donnet and Melissa Downer. I love you all and your family. To all those I forgot to thank. Charge it to my head and not my HEART. I have nothing but heartfelt gratitude and love for everyone I named and the ones I missed.

Foreword
Allison Larsen

I remember watching my oldest child take her first steps. When I felt she was ready to start walking, her dad held her, and I squatted a few short paces away and opened my arms beckoning to her. Without hesitation she began to move fearlessly towards me. She stepped forward, landing confidently on one foot before she wobbled and fell. I watched as she stuck her bottom lip out and began to sniffle. But, with encouragement she got up and tried again eventually falling into my open arms. It was an exciting time and I will never forget the proud look on her face and the celebration that followed.

Now my daughter is grown, and I help encourage a different group of people taking steps towards their goals. My clients are adults, mostly entrepreneurs, who are moving towards their business goals. The interesting thing is that we as adults are often much more hesitant to take our first steps than when we were young. We are often much harder on ourselves when we do fall, keeping us from achieving forward movement. This fear of progression and lack of movement is a huge problem that prevents people from reaching their potential and entrepreneurs from reaching ultimate success.

This is why I am so excited for this book. Shannon is a dear friend of mine who lives what he preaches. I have known him for years and have watched him stand again and again after falls. I have witnessed him moving forward despite challenges, allowing him to eventually reach massive levels of success! Now Shannon is passionate about helping others do what he did. Sometimes, just like when we fell as a child, all we need is a little encouragement to get up and keep moving towards our goals. As you read this book, you will feel encouraged to keep going in in the face of set-backs and failures. Eventually you will reach your goals if you commit to following the principles Shannon teaches.

So, get ready to be inspired to action. If you have been standing on the sideline, now is your time to stop standing and start moving. If you have fallen, now is the time to get up. You are a champion. Start moving. Keep going. Keep hustling.

Introduction

Why this book?

"You're sharp, Shannon. You could leave too," Kevin said to me as he packed up his desk and walked out of the call center. He was the 3rd employee this month that took off their headset, tossed it to the desk, and announced, "I'm done with this."

I had kept score of how many people hit rock bottom and woke up to unfulfilled dreams in this call center. It was as if this place was where mediocrity came to die.

Kevin felt frustrated as he left, so I am not sure that he understood the impact that he made on me in that moment. What Kevin said shook me awake. It had me questioning everything. "You're sharp, Shannon. You could leave too."

But what would I do? Where would I go? Where would I start? All I could think of was the reasons that had stopped me my entire life. I don't have a degree. I don't have the money. I was not raised that way. I don't have the fortune or resources to start my own business. The list goes on.

1

I have always sensed my power, brilliance, and leadership, but never developed it or evolved it. Teachers, coaches, and bosses taught me to "tone it down" growing up. I was waking up to how stifled I was and how I had accepted my own level of mediocrity.

Besides, even though Kevin's words woke me up to something new, I had no idea what I would want to do. I worked for other people my whole life. I had only ever dreamed of what was possible, but on that day, when he packed up and marched out, I knew I wasn't far behind him.

A coworker that I hardly knew showed me that I was smart and capable. Permission was all I needed. I felt the jolt that the whole world of possibility was available to me. I woke up. I chose that I was ready to figure out entrepreneurship despite any fears or insecurities I may have had. I was ready to take a leap of faith. Instead of wishing hoping and praying for luck, I knew it was time to make my own.

In that awakening moment, I became motivated to make moves that generated momentum. I was so motivated that I almost made it out the door before Kevin's exit door closed. I was ready. I wasn't clear about the path, but I was certain about the direction I wanted my life to go.

Why this book?

I left that call center job and I have been learning and growing ever since. I answered the call to fulfill the potential of my power, intelligence, and leadership. Not having a degree didn't mean a thing anymore. I registered into the school of life and hard knocks. I have taken enough hits and have bounced back time after time to bring this book to you. I have polished my skills and refined my message enough to bring you this book. I want to raise your awareness the same way Kevin did to me.

"You are sharp, and you can do it too." This book will show you how. It is your time to let go of any limiting beliefs and toss them to the side. Start making moves that will create your momentum. Together, we will dig in on what brings you to life and ignites that fire within. You will learn how to use your resources to reach levels of success that you only ever dreamt of. You will be a master of yourself. By the end of this book, you will be moving full steam towards your fullest dream.

Part I:

Foundation

Chapter 1

Distinguishing the Three M's

I want to jump start this book by welcoming you to the possibility of the next biggest shift in your life! Buckle your seat belt. By the time we get to talking about momentum, we will be moving at a hundred miles per hour! This book isn't for the faint of heart. It's for those of you ready to take on the speed and direction of your life with everything you've got!

This book has three major topics: Motivation, Movement, and Momentum.

First, we will learn the difference between the three "M's." These three powerful "M's" often get tied together and collapsed as one in the same. They do not have the same characteristics when used as different tools. Implementing the three "M's" can transform the quality of your life and the results you produce.

To cause the three "M's" to happen in your life, you must understand them. So, let's begin.

On a surface level, motivation is that energy you feel. It's the buzz of a great speech or an exhilarating experience. Motivation also stems from within. It's a fire in your heart or belly. It's a distractive string of thoughts that pull you in the direction you want to be going.

Something to know about motivation is that it doesn't last. In fact, Zig Ziglar is often quoted saying that, "motivation doesn't last. Neither does bathing." Most motivation you feel will last you the length of time of a shower. This does not mean that you are not a motivated person. It means that motivation is nothing but a feeling without movement and momentum.

Movement is an essential piece of the equation in this book and your success. Movement is the inspired action that you take when you have motivation. Without movement, motivation is icing with no cake and it leaves you with a sugar rush.

Generating movement when motivated separates the dreamers from the achievers. It makes the difference between having a dream and living your dream life. Movement *is* what sets you apart. It is what causes you to rise above. When you begin to move, you move out of your circumstance. Now you can take the physical, mental, and emotional steps forward. People wish, hope, and dream without movement. Without moving out of their circumstance they cannot realize big goals and dreams.

Making moves when motivated will generate a snowball effect of momentum. Momentum is intangible. You cannot hold it. You can feel it. It has a ground rumbling type of approach. It rolls up like a freight train that you can sense coming down the track from miles away. It gets all the way to you before its horn blares, making its presence known.

Momentum is also much like a fickle woman. She comes and goes with the attention that you give her. When you stop the movement so does the momentum. If you're not feeling motivated, she will sense it and go away. If you do not move with passion, momentum will leave you and go to the person creating movement in their life.

It's the law of physics, "an object in motion stays in motion." You must honor this universal law and use it to generate the life you want. If you think it will take care of itself, you are mistaken. If you're waiting for success to show up at your doorstep, you will always be waiting. Do not think that opportunity will plop down in your lap without you getting off the couch. I beg you to generate the life you want.

You are responsible for the quality of your life and by way of picking up this book you are ready. Now I will share with you how to tap into that motivation to cause movement. You will create a force of momentum that is as unstoppable as a freight train.

Buckle up, cause we're heading out full steam ahead.

Chapter 2

Intro to Self

Throughout this book, I am going to share a few of my own life experiences. These experiences have taught me the difference between motivation, movement, and momentum. By taking the long way around the learning curve, I have gained the knowledge and power to write this book.

Over the course of my entrepreneurial career, I have taken swings at a few different career paths. As with most entrepreneurs, I have struck out a time or two. At some point in these pages, I'll be taking you all the way back to my singing career. As a twenty-year old, I fired my singing group's forty-year old manger. I will share a few examples of how I paid big costs to learn even bigger lessons. I am going to be very transparent throughout this book. I am confident that the parts of my life will relate to something you've been through. What I share about myself can prevent you from learning the hard way.

A younger Shannon could not have written you this book. My life experiences have made it possible for me to bring you this powerful awareness. A younger Shannon might be too proud to admit some of the missed swings I have taken. What I have come to realize is that I would not be where I am without every step of my journey. Every milestone has gotten me closer to where I have wanted to be.

Life has continued to teach, refine, and grow me. When younger and motivated, I would take any opportunity that presented itself. This caused me to back track a few times to recover my losses and dwell in my lessons learned. In this evolution, I have learned to take inspired action in the direction that I am clear I want to go. This type of movement has created the momentum I had only ever wished, hoped, and dreamed of.

Over the course of my growth, I have also authored *Your Motivational Manuals: Volume 1 and 2*. Also, I bring you other motivating masters on my radio show, *The Movement*. "The 3 M's" are my mantra: motivation, movement, and momentum. Mastery is my motivator. We will never have life all figured out. Constant learning and discovering molds us into the most fulfilled version of ourselves. This book is a celebration of being where I want to be in my life. I have come to accept my deepest commitments, strongest passions, and God given gifts. I will work to impact the world and help others master themselves as well. I will empower you to do the same.

You are one in a million and I am here to support your progress and process. In this book, we are going to generate clarity around the direction that you want your life to be going! We're going get clear on what motivates, drives, directs, and inspires you. From that awareness, you will be able to generate anything you wish!

Together we will discover how understanding and utilizing the three "M's" will propel you in life. This knowledge can save you a few of my missteps along the way. I will share this knowledge with you in an authentic way to make the biggest difference in your life.

It is my commitment that you master yourself so that you may master your life. You will have crystal clarity about your deepest commitments and sharpest tools. Through self-mastery you will create the legacy that you will want to leave *while* you are here.

Chapter 3

Intro to Teaching

Something I'd like to share about my life to start this book is that I have been a teacher for most of my life. In fact, it is a huge part of my identity and one of the most major milestones in my journey.

I taught for 20 years. I began as a trumpet instructor and have also moved into piano and drums. At the peak of my teaching career, I was seeing 120 students a week! People that know my history would consider me talented and gifted in the realm of music. This music phase of my life stretched me beyond who I knew myself to be.

This book contains examples of student's lives that my teaching transformed. Even more important, these students have transformed my leadership. Because of my students I can offer more to the world! My teaching career demanded my growth and evolution as a teacher, man, leader, and human.

I found so much of my voice in teaching. It developed my confidence. Leading and teaching children in musical arts shaped my leadership abilities. By applying those learned abilities, I have mastered a way to educate thousands more. My reach goes further than I teach because of the way I have utilized momentum to create a ripple effect around me. I teach based on the way that I learn. I treat students and others as I want to be treated.

I share this because I want you to understand the person that you're learning from in this book *is* a teacher. It is in my heart to teach, train, motivate, inspire, and guide. I will treat you as one of my own in my classroom. I will care for you in these pages and beyond. I want you to win. I want you to thrive. You can create anything you choose with three simple tools and I will teach you how to do it.

Often, you will feel as if you're talking to your brother, father, or best friend. I'm going to be real with you. I'm going tell you like it is and walk with you as you figure it out.

So, as we begin this journey, I want to lay out the two cardinal rules that I share on day one of any semester with my students:

#1: The teacher is always right.

#2: When in doubt, go back to number 1.

I say this to my students with a serious face and tone on day one in the classroom. Beyond that, I always say it from laughter and love. The message I want you to receive is that I am requesting your trust from this point on. I am asking you to open your mind and heart to what I will teach you in this book. This is an invitation to unlearn your old ways. Also, you may adapt them to serve the greater vision that you hold for your life. If you plan on diving deeper into this book, you must grow beyond who you know yourself to be.

Chapter 4

Getting Unstuck

You have limitations and a self-sabotaging belief. You may have noticed that living the same way produces the same results. It may feel like "banging your head on the same wall" over and over and over. There is nothing wrong with this. But I assert that by you reading this book, you are close to changing. You can change those predictable patterns and results. You can change the success level you are currently stuck at.

Speaking of stuck, this feeling can often occur much like getting a truck stuck in the mud. You spin the wheels attempting to get out on your own. Shifting gears from drive to reverse. You continue to attempt turning the wheel left and right to wiggle free. You keep burning oil and gas as you "gun it" going nowhere. It can be tiresome and defeating to stay in this spot for too long and eventually, you will run out of gas.

Getting out of that mud on your own is not impossible. In fact, it is very probable. You can keep trying or wait it out for the mud to dry up.

You can use tools or gravel or traction pads. There are so many innovative ways to go about getting that damn truck out of the mud. The solutions are endless.

Or, you can call a tow. You can reach out for a lifeline. The lifeline can yank you right out of your personal pit in a quarter of the time and effort. I am your tow. I am here to make this whole process much simpler, easier, and even more enjoyable. So, link up, grab hold, and let's go. This book is your hitch out of the mud you are currently sinking deeper into and I am your guide.

I promise you to be real, raw, and transparent as we go through this process together. There will be many points in the book that I will ask you to grab a pen and paper. You will get all the "mud" that is locking up your gears splashed onto paper.

The completion of the exercises will clear a path through flooded and rocky terrain. The murky waters will become clear. The puddles will dry up and you will be free and clear to burn rubber as you forge forward on your path.

To practice testing your willingness to accept my support, let's jump in the mud right now! Grab a notebook that you will use for the rest of your reading and let's "get to getting." Start a fresh sheet of paper and draw a line down the middle. Label the left side, "Old Patterns" and the right side, "New Possibilities."

On the left side, begin listing those old patterns you see on repeat.

- What keeps showing up in your life?
- What relationships are you always ending up in?
- What roles do you always end up in?
- What same results are you always creating or ending up with?
- What do you allow in your life?
- What do you keep tolerating?

I could ask those questions about a million more ways. As an intelligent human you can see where I am taking you. *Keep writing* out those old patterns until you cannot see or think of any more. Leave an extra blank page for this exercise. Discover and add more patterns to this ongoing list. Continue to uncover them and add them to the list.

Next up, begin your list of new possibilities. You cannot get anywhere that you don't believe you can go. You are where you are *because* you subconsciously *believe* this is as far as you can get. Otherwise, you would be further. Don't spend too much time upset or sad about this awareness. Feeling sorry for yourself is water to dirt ... it creates the mud you get stuck in. Instead, begin writing your dreams. There is pure magic in putting your visions onto paper. It makes them more tangible immediately.

By writing out your goals and new possibilities, you begin to materialize them. So, on the right column, begin to list what you are creating:

- What do you want?
- What would it look like to get paid to be you?
- What "work" would you be excited to do every day for the rest of your life?
- What type of work or projects would generate more energy for you?
- What legacy do you want to leave?
- What impact do you want to create?

You get it. Keep answering as you go and keep this list an ongoing one throughout this book. Never stop adding, subtracting, and clarifying as you grow. Can you feel the new energy present? Can you feel the lightness of imagining all that is possible for you and your life? Can you sense the buzzing throughout your body? Can you feel the fluttering of the butterflies in your chest or stomach?

This is a process in motivation. Getting clear about what you want will have you so excited that you will burst into movement. Not only that, when what you want is on paper in front of your eyes, a road map seems to appear. You can see what goals relate to each other.

You can see which ones must come before others and how they segue way into each other. You can see the milestones that you will step upon and before you know it, you are in full blown momentum! You will be sprinting towards your goals on solid ground. You will be an unstoppable force of momentum as you chase down your dreams.

Welcome to the shift. It is great to be here with you.

Chapter 5

The Identities I Bring

I was born a twin in 1973 in the Chicago suburbs, Broadview for my fellow Chicagoans. Being born in the suburbs of Chicago in the 70's is so much of my identity. My parents raised me Blue Collar. They taught me to work hard and earn my keep. I watched my parents hustle and grind for what we had. I learned early on that life requires grit, determination, and elbow grease. Following their example was a point of pride for me. I followed suit with the "work hard" mentality. I worked my way through college from 1991 to 1994. I majored in music with a psych minor and had big dreams of making it in the music industry. Lofty aspirations and playing big started early on for me in life. I knew it required all the elbow grease I had.

I worked my way through college at Burger King. For me to have it my way, I had to serve it up "their" way! I was a full-time student working full-time, cultivating my dreams in the meantime. I learned what it meant to put yourself through college and earn your way to anything that you want in life! I learned early on what it meant to work for what you want and have never lost the lesson. I have never lost my hustle and grind.

In all those years of serving it up for others, I have learned to put myself first. I watched others drive up to the window on a Friday night, grab their order and drive off into the night. I watched families walk up, grab their grub, and go. For 5 years, I worked more than anyone else I knew because I knew my direction. I was playing the long game. I was playing for keeps.

A major lesson I learned in my time at BK was to serve myself and then serve others from a full, whole, and complete heart! You cannot pull others up unless you stand on higher ground! Working there paid my way through school and I had the opportunity to chase my dreams because of it! Realizing that I can do full-time school and full-time work taught me a lot about myself and my capability. Accepting whatever work that came my way showed me so much of my potential.

Only by doing it, I learned that working hard for others wasn't what I wanted to do. I *had* to work for others to learn that lesson! I learned it well. It took a lot of "hard work" and time given to others for me to accept that this isn't how I want to spend my time and energy. I knew this fact so clearly that I became driven to make it on my own from a very young age!

My singing group that I had during college gave me my first great experience of chasing a dream. We were young up and comers and our following grew. The singing group had my brother and some other great friends. We sang at churches, competitions, festivals, and more. You name the venue and we were there. Even outside of my group, I would fill in as a male voice for other groups and at concerts. I sang in choirs and churches. I wrote songs and music for others and I would play trumpet wherever I could get a note in. I was doing everything imaginable! I was doing everything within my power to cross over into stardom. You name it, I was doing it! I would visualize our singing group making it big time! I visualized myself landing big gigs, offers, and record deals. I was bright eyed and bushy-tailed about my musical career. I wasn't always the most talented on stage, but I could guarantee you that I was the hardest working. I was willing to go farther to outlast any challenge we came up against. It is with this group that I got my first lesson in being a leader.

I had so many experiences in that group that taught me what it was like to work and to stand for your greatest worth. I'll never forget one of the most valuable learning experiences we had singing at a talent show. Pitched to us as a gig for a school, we registered for this school hosted talent show. The talent show hosted over 20 acts. Not what we were expecting at all and this became more obvious by the minute. It was a talent show and not an actual performance like we had thought. Nonetheless, we were there and as they say, "the show must go on!"

So, as you can imagine with 20 acts going on starting at 8pm, the show went until 4:00 am. Yes, you read that right 4am…in the morning! Every group got up, did their skit, and filed through. Finally, at some odd hour of the morning, we absolutely rocked an a cappella number! We knew we were the best in the competition. To be frank, there was no competition. We were performers coming to a school talent show, not performing for the students and staff.

We were leaps and bounds ahead of those participating for a fun evening. Some of them performing on stage for the first time. That said, we did our thing, rocked our show, and made it to the top 3. To our dismay we came in 2nd behind a teacher's magician in which the prize money ended up going back to the school.

When we thought it was in all-for-nothing kind of evening, we realized we had caught the ear of one of the judges. The judge represented a major record label. Immediately following the performance, he wanted to speak to our manager. "You guys have really got something going on," he praised. "I'd like to talk to your manager about a demo deal. Where is he?"

I pointed out our manager and away to a classroom they went. Finally! Our big break! The moment of truth! This is how it happens, right?!? I could see the headlines as I watched the two of them walk away: "Hidden Gems Discovered at Local Talent Show!" I could feel it in my bones.

While our manager negotiated the demo project, we talked about headlining shows. We sat and dreamed until we began to wonder when our manager was going to tell us when our plane for LA leaves. As time passed, our curiosity grew. What on earth could take so long to talk numbers, shake hands, and start packing?

The extra 40 something minutes they were off negotiating felt like an eternity! It was now reaching morning hours! "Where are they!?!" we kept asking each other as we sat around on the edge of the make-shift platform stage. The minutes got longer as the time got closer and closer to my Burger King shift before my classes. At that point, my eyes grew tired and my temper got short.

After what seemed like an eternity, the agent and our manager emerged from down the hall. I noticed there was no pep in their step like they had come to an agreement. Without many words, the judge said a half-hearted good bye and took half of my heart with him. "What the hell happened?!?!?" we all asked the second the judge left ear shot.

Immediately, he started dissing the agent for not offering us triple the rate for our first demo. "He wanted to offer us $***** and I asked for $*****. It wasn't enough! You guys deserve more than that!" our manager answered. That agent offered us a demo project for more money than I had ever seen in my life.

We lost the opportunity. We stood there shocked. All our jaws had dropped. We pulled it together and began to question him. He wanted more money. We got turned away because he demanded a higher rate.

We lost the opportunity because he had asked for a higher rate without consulting us. Remember how I mentioned the original offer was more money than we had ever seen? It made me so upset to see an opportunity like that come straight to us and slip out of someone else's hands.

It was infuriating. It was defeating. It took all the wind out of our sails. To add insult to injury, this experience happened 2 more times before I had lost my patience. I had to step up as the leader of the group. We had grabbed the attention and admiration of over 3 major record labels. We let the opportunities walk away by trusting someone else to negotiate our worth. I couldn't stand for it anymore. After three strikes, I couldn't take it anymore. We were all suffering due to someone else's greed and I wouldn't stand for it anymore. I fired the manager and sent him on his way.

We knew that we wanted to make it in music even if it meant getting our foot in the door. We were fine starting from square one and working ourselves up as opposed to make it big right away. Most of those offers *were* the same as making it big and they had gotten away. They had gotten far away at this point.

Firing our manager and trying to make it on our own damaged our morale. Not seeing eye to eye on so many levels caused breakdowns in trust and lack of unity. Discouragement about our lack of success followed.

In 1995 the group we had created over 4 year disbanded. We all went our separate ways. A few of them stuck together and tried to reinvent themselves. I too took a route of reinvention. I began vocal and piano lessons at Dora Lynn Academy in Oak Park. I entered the doors as a student and never knew it would evolve the way that it did. Shortly after enrolling into the Academy, the invitation came to volunteer and teach. I accepted a teaching position at the

Academy with gratefulness. Teaching afforded me the opportunity to grow my personal and professional skills. I would work a day job and jet over to teach trumpet, piano, and drum lessons to children and young adults.

I volunteered so much of my life there for 20 years! So many times, people would ask me how or why I do it. I can say it was never a chore. I never remember a day having to drag myself there. It brought me joy and it gave me passion and purpose!

I loved what I was doing at Dora Lynn Academy. I loved the impact I made. Teaching at Dora Lynn Academy shaped me into a better person. Teaching others surfaced so many of my own passions. This experience surfaced my self-worth and I discovered my voice in it!

This phase of my life taught me how capable I am and what my purpose is for my time on Earth! I have loved every part of teaching and I have brought it to you in a new way in the form of this book! It was only by evolving through that process that I found my voice and power in speaking. I found confidence in what I am bringing to you today.

You will meet many of my identities such as the lead singer and musician. You will meet the teacher and the educator. Also, you will meet the employer and the unemployable.

You will meet so many different identities that I have taken on throughout my life. I am bringing them all to you to teach you the lessons learned. You will learn from my missteps. You will learn from my strides and leaps that I have taken towards my fullest life!

I am bringing you everything I've got to support you in going for everything you want! Buckle up, we are about to have a bunch of fun.

Chapter 6
The Cycle of Mastery

I want to bring a concept to you to consider as we move forward in our journey together of living our fullest lives. Motivation, Movement, and Momentum exist in a triangle formation as a cyclical concept. Energy goes from one to the other. Draw out this triangle on a sheet of paper. Hang it somewhere that you will see it often while reading this book. Go ahead, grab the paper…I'll wait…

Great! Now go ahead and draw that triangle. Label the top angle Motivation. The bottom right angle will be Movement. Can you guess the bottom left? Right on! Label that last one Momentum and begin to trace the triangle clockwise. Say the words aloud, "Motivation-Movement-Momentum, Motivation-Movement-Momentum." You can even add a little tune to it when you start feeling it. You can bob your head and tap your foot to it. Create a jingle of it if it serves you but get used to this cycle.

You see, when you have motivation, you generate movement, and it creates momentum. Momentum creates more motivation. Motivation creates more movement and it goes on and on. It builds and builds. It adds and multiplies.

YOU have control over this cycle. You can start and stop it at any time. When you begin to believe in it, you create the momentum of a freight rolling down the tracks. Your speed will catch a pace that would become unstoppable in the face of obstacles. YOU will become unstoppable in the face of obstacles.

Did your heart start to race as you read that? Yeah. It's because you're hungry. You are ready to level up in life. You are ready to have your dreams become your reality. I get it. I know because I am you. I have been at the point in my life where my visions were nothing but day dreams at the desk of a call center.

I get the passion burning inside of you. The embers that smothered your heart caught flame. Welcome to your awakening. Welcome back to your consciousness. We are taking life to the next level and beyond.

As we take a high-speed journey through this book, I will share how to harness the power of the 3 M's as a tool for success. The Cycle of Mastery will have you mastering life. That includes relationships, projects, health, wealth, and more. This knowledge and awareness will empower you to create a life you love.

I will be with you along the way to break this cycle down. The Cycle of Mastery will make clear what to do as you put your hands on the steering wheel of your life. We will get our hands dirty, break a little sweat, and construct your best life. No matter where you're starting and no matter where you're going, *it's all about never stopping.*

I am only introducing this concept to you to start the book and it will show up time and time again as you read on. When you buy into it, you will see it show up again and again all over your life! Get very present and aware of The Cycle of Mastery and begin to practice it. Before you even realize what happened, you will be mastering your life!

Chapter 7
Book of Promise

The most authentic commitment is to have others believing that they *can*. I am here to say "Yes! You can!" and to ask, "What are you waiting on?" So, while I will cheer you on, I will also kick you in the pants to "get to getting!"

I have found so much of my own motivation in proving others wrong when they tell me I can't. I have felt so proud when proving myself right that I can in fact do what I dream of. It is my goal to show you that you can also do it. I watch too many students of mine struggle with having no one in their corner. Too many of these youngsters grew up believing that they don't have anything to look forward to.

Teaching revealed a gap in this world that I realized my heart could fill. Since coming to this realization, I have accepted the calling to chase my biggest dreams. I want to prove to others that we can do anything we set our minds to. This mentality drove me to write the *Motivation Manuals 1 and 2* and now bring this book to you.

I am willing to reveal myself and my life lessons to have you discover some of your own! Believe in the principle of plenty. There is room for everyone at the top. There is no limit to success. We may all have it all.

I know that you are here because you are looking for a way. I am here to light your fire. I am here to tell you how exactly you can achieve what you want. Use this book for everything that it is worth. I am bringing you decades of lessons and experience. You will have the benefit of seeing my tragedies and triumphs. Use this book as your guide to pave your way to every next level of your life.

I have come way too far to stop now. I have seen too many people in life suffer from limitations that they place on themselves! We are going to spend a ton of this book breaking up those limitations. By the end of this process, you will be bursting past the barriers of your comfort zone. Accept your greatness and go full throttle!

We are going to generate your motivation, movement, and momentum. You will be moving at the speed of light. You will break the sound barrier. You will burst through rejection and disappointment. You will be unstoppable by the barriers that had once kept you trapped.

By the end of this book you will hardly recognize that old version of you. You will have discovered so much more greatness in yourself. You will realize your full capability and you will develop the courage to use it!

Part II:

Discover and Shift

Chapter 8

Two Kinds of People: Resistance

There are two kinds of people in this world. People who can sense change and step right into it and those who resist it. I'm going to spend most of this chapter talking to those of you who resist the change that you can sense. It's that nagging feeling tapping you on the shoulder year after year decade after decade.

It is so natural for us as humans to desire predictability and consistency. We associate that with safety. We love security and a sense of control. Yet, desire will keep us stuck and wrapped up inside our comfort zones. In our comfort zones we suffer from anxiety and self-doubt. This can be a tragic event.

Most everyone's advice on their deathbed is about regrets. They wish they would have "gone for it" more. They wish they had cared less about what other people thought of them and gone for it more. Suffering from their regrets, they feel the sting of not having lived their fullest life.

It is when we resist change that we struggle. Attempting to halt a law of nature will stop you and your progress. If you haven't heard the quote yet, allow me to be the one to share, "the only thing that is consistent in life is change." The more used to evolution you become the more that comes available to you. More possibility opens-up for you to tap into.

So, for those of you who resist the natural change, I invite you to begin opening your mind and heart to it. Otherwise, you cannot use the force of change to create momentum. I learned this lesson when the music school closed. I can say that if it weren't for that school closing its doors, I would still be teaching music to this day. I wasn't ready or willing.

I had no desire for change. I could sense it sometimes. I could somewhat tell that I was outgrowing my role. Yet, I loved it. I never tired of it. I knew that there was more for me. For so long, I struggled with many doubts about what was next for me.

I loved the validation of being a teacher and impacting my students. I wanted nothing more than to know I was making a difference in this world for people and their futures. My whole mission is to have people understand and be able to announce, "I can!"

We can do anything we want. We can achieve anything we want, and we can go for

37

anything we want. While uncovering this mission, I caught myself not doing the things that I was preaching at this point. The school shut-down caused me to breakdown. I love things staying the same.

The consistency was like a security blanket for me. Many of you sit in a consistent situation that feels cozy. Know that there's more for you, and I invite you to accept that call and move. Only by having the school close and that position taken away from me did I begin to sort through the thoughts. I thought, "what's next for my life?" The teaching position did not exist. I could not turn back. For a short moment, I felt the loss. There was this huge void in my life created by this school closing its doors. It was the first time that I was looking into my future not knowing what came next. I would be stepping onward without a real clue about it. It wasn't like jumping off a cliff or building and parachute your way down. It was like getting kicked off the cliff and clawing at the passing air, praying for a lifeline or a helicopter.

It scared the hell out of me! This major shift caused a lot of breakdowns before it caused my breakthroughs. I began searching for what was next for me. I got more serious about what was available and the opportunities and people in my life. It had me looking beyond my current circumstances. "What could I create for myself?"

Working on something new got me into movement. I was standing dead still before that school closed-down. I had the motivation to make a difference, but I wasn't moving in the right direction. I needed to change direction to create enough momentum to reach my highest potential. For those of you resisting that change or resisting your greatness, listen to the call of your heart. Your heart will reveal what's next for you. Honor those urges. Honor those whispers of your heart.

Chapter 9

Intrinsic vs Extrinsic

I love to teach the difference between intrinsic and extrinsic motivation. Intrinsic motivation is the motivation that comes from within. It is real. It is genuine. It is your own. It is not produced outside of you and it never goes away!

Think about it in this moment. Think about the dreams that you've always had even from youth. Think about the natural talents and skills that you have. Consider the things that you love and energize you. This is all intrinsic

It's who you are it's what makes you the *person you are,* and it will never leave or go away. Often in the course of our lives, our intrinsic motivation gets piled up on. It gets buried down there so deep that we forget about it. We lose access to it. When we lose access, we lose a sense of self. Our intrinsic motivation is the root of who we are. When we forget who we are, what we love, or what we're motivated by, we began to lose our sense of purpose.

Intrinsic motivation is essential to finding and unleashing the fullest version of you! To take your career to the next level you must know what the heck you give a damn about! You must rediscover who you know yourself to be. It requires peeling back the many layers of disappointments and mistakes. Remember who you are, where you come from, and where you're headed.

Your intrinsic motivation is essential to your movement and momentum. If you choose to chase dreams that are outside of you, you will always be chasing. You will catch one thing and create another one to chase. When you chase relationships and status, you will find yourself unfulfilled.

It is vital that you peel back the layers of life. If buried, allow your intrinsic motivation to surface. Let that motivation bubble up and rise to the surface of your heart. Let that inspired heart explode from it. This is where you will find your next and natural inspired action to take.

On the other side of the same coin is extrinsic motivation. This is all those accolades, trophies, titles, awards, money, houses and cars. Now, don't get me wrong those things are wonderful. I can admit to you that I shoot for those goals myself. Yet, they are not the thing that has me choose my life purpose or the direction of my life. They are bi-products of honoring my intrinsic motivation.

I know what I love to do. I know what I'm great at. I know what I'm passionate about and I know the impact I want to have on this world and the legacy that I want to leave. My intrinsic motivation drives me. My extrinsic motivation is a reward for honoring what my heart is telling me.

To further clarify, the extrinsic motivation of the shiny "things" come and go. None of them last. They fade. They rot. They disintegrate. They get lost or taken. Do not place too much emphasis or value on extrinsic motivation. Your self-worth may go away with the shiny things.

Take out a sheet of paper. Draw a line right down the middle. On one side of the line write down your intrinsic motivators. On the other side write a list of extrinsic motivators. Understand the difference between the two. Nothing is wrong with either. Nothing at all. You can love money. You can love the big house and the cars. You can soak up the accolades. Don't lean on them because when they drive off, you will tip over.

After writing it out, take a good look at that list of intrinsic motivation and lean into *that*. Get that *this* is who you are, and this is the legacy that you will leave. Hang your hat on the difference that you will make in this world. You can create extrinsic motivation time after time after time. The excitement comes when you continue to create and generate outside of you. You are so present to what is inside of you.

Chapter 10

Enthusiasm vs Excitement

Close to intrinsic and extrinsic motivation is the difference between enthusiasm and excitement. Rooted deep within you, enthusiasm is a true passion. Enthusiasm is a passion for what it is that you want to do and the difference that you want to make. Excitement is the way that your enthusiasm shows up outside of your body, or as an expression.

Consider that you may commit to something that you love. On certain days you have way more excitement about it than other days. You may have a commitment to educating youth and some days you show up more excited than others. You want to make a difference with your nonprofit. Some days it takes a little more fuel in the tank to show up with your authentic passion.

Your enthusiasm never goes away. It is yours. You measure excitement by your energy level and by the people in your life.

Something that is very cool is that you can choose your excitement level. This is often referred to as "fake it till you make it." It's like smiling until you're happy. The muscles of the face recognize a smile and it will shift your mood when you hold a smile long enough. You can do this with excitement. Your enthusiasm surfaces into the mind. If you turn your excitement up on purpose, you can generate your own motivation! Your enthusiasm is always there. Your mind and body wait for you. And I'm very excited for you to get to use this awareness on purpose!

If we waited for an increase in our excitement level to act, we'd be stuck, frustrated, and feeling held back by life. Get clear about your enthusiasm and begin jumping into your fullest life.

For the better part of my life, I have been an educator. Even though my discipline was music, I love educating in every sense of the craft. So much of *who* I am is "teacher" and it brings me to life. From mentorship to friendship, impacting others makes my spirit come alive. Like I have said before, there was never a day I had to drag myself into the classroom. I never grow tired of making a difference in the lives of others. My commitment to changing this world through impacting others is my intrinsic motivation. It lives inside of me.

Making a difference and transforming a life is an extrinsic factor for me. The validation of recognition is outside of me. Watching students perform on stage in front of their parents is external. There are so many things that teachers link their worth to. When those "signs of success" stop showing up as evidence, it can diminish purpose and passion.

Purpose and passion add energy to extrinsic and intrinsic motivation. Lack of signs of success cause doubt. Doubt diminishes purpose and passion. As you can tell, this is where motivation can begin to wither away like air from a balloon. It's a slow leak and a slow sink until that balloon is shrunken and withered on the floor, never to float again.

Chapter 11
Prioritizing

We understand prioritizing as something important. Prioritizing is one of the single most important things you can do for your motivation.

For example, you can work 20 hours each day on something that you have passion for. Passion for the work gives you energy. You can work for 2 hours on something that you can't stand, and it would exhaust you to your core. I know that you know this is true.

I advocate living a balanced life that includes rest and self-care. There is no limit to the motivation and energy when you work on something you love. You continue to work on the things you love. Prioritizing your passions is vital to your motivational level. If you get stuck or exhausted, lean more towards your passions.

It is time that you take ownership over your priority list. Now, I invite you to rank health, career, relationship, money, religion, and feel free to add more. Put them in and most important to least important priority list that you *want* to see them. On the other side of outline, put them into the priority list as they exist today. How does your priority lists compare?

This is the time to get real with yourself. You're the only one living your life. You're on your own until you engage others in what you are up to. You can keep lying about your priorities or you can get real. You can create motivation that will cause the movement that you're ready to make. Reading this book is no mistake even if you feel like you're bursting at the seams with new awareness.

It's your time already! In case it hasn't sunken in yet, hear me now. Quit waiting! Now is your time! Nothing will ever be perfect, and you'll always have a hundred excuses. It's easy to kick back on your goals and the world will allow you to have your excuses. Unlike those still wishing and waiting, I am here for you and with you. I am here to call you forth past what has stopped you.

Feeling like a victim of my circumstances had stopped me in my life. I shared with you in the introduction that I had been awakened. Awakened into my greatness by the simple reflection that I had the ability to live a life I love. I am here to speak loud and clear to you that it is possible for you too.

Prioritizing

Give up anything that doesn't serve your greater purpose. Focus on your life in a way that will create your movement, and momentum, and begin to do that. Now is your time.

Chapter 12

Discovering Your Deepest Commitment and Your Sharpest Tool

Educating humans to live their best lives is something that brings me to life on so many levels.

As I grew in education my voice evolved. I remember showing up on days and speaking to them about more than music. I was experiencing the power of my voice growing. I preached confidence to them. I grew my own as I grew theirs. Being a father AND brother figure in their eyes gave me a sense of self. I discovered so much of myself in their eyes and hearts.

The more I spoke, the more I developed my voice. It had a boom and a rumble when revved up with passion. It shook roots and foundations. Over the course of time, I had truly come to discover that my voice was my sharpest tool. My voice served the deepest commitment I have of making a difference in this world.

As I have evolved over time, I have learned to use my voice in different ways. It has gone through phases of authenticity. When I took on merchant services and real estate, I was learning entrepreneurship. Thus, the focus on my authenticity and voice did not rank high on my priority list. I became focused on how to make it. The distraction of earning money and growing a business caused me to lose a little bit of my motivation.

Investing without a return on investment took the wind out of my sails. I lost my sense of purpose, my voice, and my motivation.

I received a call from a grandma of one of my most disruptive students. Her call reminded of the difference that I make in the lives of children. This grandma shook me awake the same way as the guy from the call center. This grandma shook me awake to the difference I made for her grandson.

I haven't always honored my call to be the one for others. For so many years while trying to figure stuff out for myself, I had been focused on what my next step was. I was more focused on what I should do about my situations and how I will succeed in life. As I have grown, especially while teaching children, I have seen the true impact of who I am.

In 2007 I had kicked Julian out of class for about the 15th time in 10 weeks. His smart mouth and quick-witted attitude challenged my authority and patience. We had a dynamic relationship in which we went back and forth like father and son. He would speak out, I would correct him. I would misspeak and immediately he would call me on it without missing a beat. He got on every nerve I had.

He had finally tipped the scale on what I was willing to tolerate. I overheard him talk back to another student's parent under my watch. Not more than a minute later, I kicked him out of my class and sent him packing home. If there's one thing I will not tolerate, it is disrespect toward elders. Not for a second.

After I kicked him out and told him he wouldn't be coming back to my class I heard from his grandmother, Loretta. She met me at school the very next lesson to ask me to have Julian back in my class. I explained to her that there was "no way, no how" about having Julian back in my class to disrupt even one more time.

He had wasted every chance I ever wanted to give him and sure that there was no difference I was making in his life. He seemed committed to being resistant, defiant, and speak without thinking. Once he had turned that behavior on another student's parent, I had had enough. I was not willing to budge on this.

Discovering Your Deepest Commitment and Your Sharpest Tool

Even in my frustration, I couldn't avoid what Julian's grandmother was asking me. She begged with tears welling up in her eyes, "Please have him back in your class Mr. Hughes!" She said with her voice cracking, "Mr. Hughes, you are the only male figure that makes the difference for him."

I didn't want to believe it. I didn't want to accept the responsibility of being the only positive male figure in this young man's life. After all, he was a pain in my ass. Yet, there was no way that I could turn my back on him at this point. Her heartfelt request pulled every one of my heart strings. This was the day that I accepted my responsibility as the gift that I am. It was in that moment that I allowed Julian back into my classroom.

I understood my role in this young man's life, and I accepted to the invitation to step into a new phase of leadership. I stepped into "fatherhood" of sorts. I've never had a problem being firm, clear, and authoritative with my students. Yet, this grandmother's request called me higher.

It was this day that I accepted how big I knew I would become. In this book and in life, I am bringing to you father, brother, and friend to bring you closer to your dreams. I am bringing you everything I know to get you where you are going with motivation, movement, and momentum. I get that if you are reading this book, I get to be The One for you and your powerful transition in life. I am honored and humbled to be here with you.

Grandma Loretta reminded of the difference that I make in the lives of others, young and old. With the voice that I have and a heart that cares, I have become hell bent on utilizing my gifts. As my mission I commit to serve from a full heart. I became realigned with what I am up to and I began to honor my voice. My deepest commitment is to make a difference. My voice is my sharpest tool.

Chapter 13

Entrepreneurial Mindshift

There was a time in my 20's where I began to think outside the box. You already know I put in long hours. And with very little sleep in college, I "bounced" from books to burgers to back-stages. I was raised up to have a solid work ethic and sacrifice for the dream. I saw my parents work and sacrifice as both employees and entrepreneurs. Their work ethic is engrained into me. In so many ways, I followed their example of hard work and living right.

As a youngster, I noticed the hard work. I saw the sacrifice and long hours. The hustle and grind that went into making it was seen at a young age and I picked up their habits and belief systems. I walked in their footsteps all the way through college.

I worked hard, lived pay check to pay check, and traded my hours for dollars. I worked to live up to what I thought my parents expected of me. I was proud to be doing what I thought I had seen my parents doing; earning an honest wage. Over time, the more I did this the louder the conversation got in the back of my head. "This doesn't fit me." I could hear, "There's more to life than this." I could hear this in my head and feel it in my heart. This was a truth in every fiber of my being. I could sense this and yet, I knew no other way.

I did know that I wouldn't be spending decades living and working for approval from others. There was a part of me that knew I could work smarter than harder. Life didn't have to be a struggle or constant uphill climb. This new way of being began to force its way through with or without my agreement or preparedness. It was an internal truth rising-up and forcing its way out of me. I couldn't avoid it. The idea of doing something different became more appealing by the minute.

My arising desires, thoughts, and urges seemed somewhat scary. They seemed unpredictable and yet, I couldn't seem to deny it. Resisting it caused a relentless thought pattern of evolution, innovation, and growth. When I thought about my future, I saw a man on stage with a microphone in his hand. The man in my vision had hair on his head but that is beside the point. A few years went by with this small flame growing inside of me. Even though I could sense it, I was having a hard time really gaining clarity about what it all meant. What direction should I go? No matter the resistance, I had to honor the shift occurring in my mind set.

As I phased in to my thirty's, I began to create what it would be like to work for myself. I knew I had all the motivation required to create an amazing life. What was evident in my life was the fact that I was only dreaming about it. I fantasized about a day that I'd work for myself and retire early. In my fantasy I'd motivate and impact thousands. It became clearer that all I was doing was dreaming of the next chapter of my life. I knew that it would only come to fruition through movement. It was time to get to "stepping."

The time had come to reevaluate. Did I want to work for somebody else the rest of my life or step outside of my comfort zone? I chose the latter and began stepping towards my dreams! This next quarter of the book, I am going to walk with you as you take the next steps of your journey. I am going to support you in creating your best life. Your thoughts will become things. Your dreams will become your current situation. Your current situation will reflect what you say that you want!

Get ready, get set, get your mentors!

Start your engines, folks! It is your time to get out of your own way! I will tell you first hand that I have been on every end of the spectrum of sharing my dreams and goals! I was one of those people who would be so excited about a new venture or idea. I would announce what I was up to constantly. I would tell people all my visions and dreams. Over time, I shifted into one of those people who would keep my dreams to myself. I would hide out about them. I have been all over the board and so wherever you're at, I get you. Yet, you have the decision to share your goals and dreams. I want to give you a few bits of information and inspiration. How do you share your dream so that you can get support and get closer to your goal?

A few different things will happen when you share your dreams and goals. You will have the naysayers. You will have the friends and family in your life who tell you that you're dreaming too big. The size and scale of your dreams will make them uncomfortable. They will tell you to slow down, give it up, get real, or flat out wake the hell up.

Many times, people can't dream as big as you because they're jaded by their own past or disappointments. That is none of your business. Your business is your business. Your success is your business. Your job is to bring your dreams, visions, and goals to reality. You do this by delivering on the God given gifts, skills, and talents that you were born with.

Don't sweat the naysayers. They have their own struggles they're dealing with. Have compassion for them and leave them right where they're at to doubt, question, blame, and judge. That is not for you to fix and that is not for you to figure out. Oddly enough, they come around after you start succeeding anyways. That is a syndrome of the naysayers. They must see before they believe and that is not you. You are already a believer in yourself, God, and your potential. The more energy you spend on the naysayers, the less time and energy you spend thriving in your business. Let the negativity go and move forward!

Another experience that may happen while sharing your dreams is that you put your own foot in your mouth. You talk big games from a spurt of motivation but then you don't execute the movements. You must execute the movements! We will spend the next part of this book talking about execution, so that you can remove your foot from your mouth.

If you dream something big and you want to tell people about it, make sure that you're willing to do whatever it takes. Are you willing to go through the struggles? Can you turn trials into triumphs? Do you have the will to turn tribulations into celebrations? Get crystal clear about what it would take to make your dream a reality. Make sure that you are willing to weather the storm before you go shouting it from rooftops.

Also, in the movement section, we will be generating Roadmaps to get you super clear and inspired. This will be a great opportunity to gauge if it's a dream that you want to share with people. Complete a Roadmap around your vision. You can get support for the direction that you're taking your life. If you commit to the goal and vision, share it! Tell the town, alert the media, and call your Momma about it! Let the people know because at this point, it becomes just a matter of time before you have it.

Turning your thoughts into things can go wrong a thousand times over. When you decide your vision will be reality, you might as well set it in stone. You will become unstoppable with your Roadmap in hand. You will be taking inspired action left and right. This movement will create momentum. The Cycle of Mastery will have you creating a whirlwind of results!

Beyond sharing your goals, you will want to get mentors and coaches that will support you. Let me tell you, none of us get to where we're going alone. You can try and try and try to roll solo all-the-day long. This will have you feeling isolated, alone and unsupported. You'll feel like people are doubting or judging you. You haven't shared your dream to get the appropriate support that you need.

Getting the appropriate coaches and mentors *makes* the difference between success and failure. I am going to take solo off the table right away. In my example, I cannot be a success as a speaker as a one man show. I have a team of coaches, producers, writers, managers, schedules, and so on. I could not succeed solo. Solo would mean I have no listeners. I would have no guests at my events. I wouldn't have any participants in my courses. Clear? Great. Give up the solo show and start finding your team.

Let's talk about getting a powerful team that moves and generates momentum with you. When we start out trying to save a few bucks, we get what we pay for. The best place to invest your money right away is in your education and guidance. That is the investment that will grow you and your income at the same time. Do not cut corners with coaches.

If you hire a naysayer to get you where you're going, you might as well give it all up right now. You would already be giving up your money and then they will deplete your energy and motivation. If you hired them because they are cheap or "free" the cost will be your success. Do *not* cut corners here. Get a coach or mentor that is further down the path than you. They will know their value and they will know their rate. Pay it. It is not a payment to them, it is an investment in yourself. It is you putting your money down on you. You are worth it, and your life is worth it. Your dream is worth it.

Now, there are plenty of other strategies and practices for success you must take on. Of course, I will be sharing those throughout the book. Finding the right support for you is one of the most important moves you will make in your business. Hands down, the most effective strategy is the help that you hire! Hiring the right coach is like Goldilocks finding the right porridge. Having people that you jive with and that you can relate to makes the difference in your success.

I have hired plenty of amazing coaches who don't resonate with me and our time together is usually short. Hiring the right coaches have taken me leaps and bounds in life. I am sharing this awareness so that you can take advantage of it and save yourself a few bucks. Hiring the right people and support systems right away makes good business sense.

Know the way that you learn. Understand the way you respond to certain coaching styles. Get clear about the kind of person and entrepreneur that you are so that the perfect guide can enter your life. From there, open yourself to learning. Become willing to discover new ways of getting what you want. Make sure that you are coachable, so that you can learn things. Your coach will teach you principles about entrepreneurship and life. Many lessons learned will collapse time frames to achieving your goals.

Having a mentor is essential! Ask any coach or entrepreneur and they will admit that "coaches have coaches." Oprah Winfrey had 5 life coaches while building her empire. Tony Robbins has a giant team around him. Anybody with notable success has gotten there with the support and guidance of a team.

None of us are any better alone. We are better together. When you live this principle, you will go far. In fact, if you want to speed-up the process, you can go by yourself but if you want to go far, you must get a team. By answering the questions below you will start the team building process:

- What sort of energy do I have?
- What kind of person do I work best with?
- What kind of person do I not want to work with?
- What is my learning style?
- How do I like to be pushed and coached?
- How do I like to be talked to?
- How do I talk to others?
- How open am I to being coached?
- What am I resistant to?

- What gaps and weakness do I have that a coach could support?
- What is missing and what kind of person can I see myself working with to create it?

As we shift into the movement section of this book, accept me as your coach. I am and will continue to guide you in the direction that you are taking your life. It is no mistake at all that you found this book and that my guidance found you. It is perfect timing for whatever you are up to. Trust the process and step into it with purpose. I am here to guide you to that next level and beyond.

Part III:

Next Level and Beyond

Chapter 14

Starting

Before we talk about movement, we must talk about starting! You will hear the same advice in different ways from different speakers or books. To get to your destination, you start by taking the first step.

I could end this whole part of the book with that fact. Yet, if that much advice worked, it would have worked by now. In fact, you know that point and you are still standing still wondering about how to start.

There is nothing more to it. There's never a right time. There is never a right moment without an action that makes you different. You don't ever have the proper training. You don't need more degrees first. You need to start!

Starting will reveal the training that you need. It will reveal where you are now and the gap between where you are now and where you want to be. There is no way of knowing without starting and by doing so, you create that movement. You create the next step and the next and the next.

Something to know about those steps is you can't take one without the other. Writing my first book gave me the opportunity to host my own radio show. My teaching experiences led into writing books. I would not have gotten teaching experience without my singing group in college.

Life does occur as a staircase and while you can try like hell to skip steps, you can only skip a few at the max. You can only skip as many steps that your legs will reach. Same goes for your mind and your heart. You can only jump as many steps as your capacity can take you. There are some steps that you must stand on longer while you get use to that elevation.

There is growth that must happen by evolution. I had to get experience from things that had already happened to take the next step of experience. Meaning that you can give up being perfect from jump street. Allow yourself room to grow into what you are creating step by beautiful step.

You must start. Start the next project. Take one action on the next goal and it will move you to the next. One of the most important parts about movement is that you learn to enjoy every step. You realize how one step leads to the other. This is where momentum comes, but we will get to that later. I find it quite entertaining how movement led to momentum even in this paragraph. You will come to see that movement, even in the wrong direction can cause momentum. That is why it is so important to understand the motivation section of this book and your heart.

There are too many times that I had started without thinking something through. I am dumb enough to try anything once and because of it, I have learned to decipher what is worth sticking with. I've paid all the money. I've spent all the hours. I've given all my energy. I have given things away. I've taken what I've can for free. I have spun about every wheel hoping and ready to hit the jackpot and so often, it has cost me my savings.

Movement without clarity can shave years off your life and hairs off your head. Trust me. Check the book cover. I have sacrificed my hair for your benefit in this book. I'm going you tell a few stories of my starting and moving to save you a few missteps.

No matter how insightful I am, there are some lessons that you will learn on your own. I can tell you 10 ways to Sunday and there are a few things that you'll have to try to figure out. This is true especially when it comes to starting and running your own business. There are going to be things that you learn by trial-and-error.

I will share as many tips and tricks as I can for you. Until you start creating your own movement, you'll never know what it feels like to learn that lesson. I learned from mentors like Tony Robbins by asking a million questions in a row. I learned to do this to save myself in my journey of entrepreneurship.

I will share many of the lessons that I have learned from many great people. I have spent thousands of dollars learning and wrapping it up for you in this package. Use it for what it's worth. Yet, I don't know that I can say it enough times, you must get started. You must create your own movement. You must follow where your heart is pulling you so that you can to live your dreams.

Chapter 15
Movement

An object in motion stays in motion. It works for the law of physics, but our human minds can mangle this up. As we do with everything, we tend to over complicate. We want to stay comfortable in the "motivation phase." We have difficulty crossing into movement. Watch for and catch yourself doing this. It can be detrimental to your goals, vision, clarity, and motivation. It will cost you your dreams.

Motivation is a lot like fireworks. It looks and feels exciting but there's nothing to them once the crackle disappears. When it comes to movement, there is traction. Your wheels are spinning, and you are covering ground with each rotation. Movement gets you from point A to point B. It makes a difference in your scenery and it can drive you to a new climate. It can elevate you to a new level.

Movement can happen in a lot of different ways. Different phases of your life and business has movement. Movement can look like walking through a front door and shaking a hand. Opening a laptop, picking up a phone, or swiping a card indicates movement. Movement can look like saying yes, saying no, and saying thank you. Movement is measurable. Movement produces results.

Each move creates the next. Even when you take a misstep, there is movement that produces a result and a new awareness. There are no wrong moves, only lessons. You can always take a step back to recalibrate your plan of action. Without movement though, you have no reference of what works for you and what doesn't. You will always catch yourself wondering about the next right thing to do instead of finding out. Movement creates evidence and proof.

Check this out. Movement is market research. When you are launching a product or service, you must get it in the market. You must move it from your head to the physical reality and then to the consumers! That motion will then teach you about what the 2.0 version should include and exclude.

Consider yourself as the example of this. Each year, very likely around New Year's or your birthday, you review your year, yourself, and your life. You do some analyzing of the previous year's movement, or lack thereof.

From this evaluation, you refine and release 3.0 and 4.0....and 50.0.

Instead of sitting in motivation mode or fake enthusiasm mode, get your life off the ground! Launch that biz. Write that book. Release that product. Share your service and give up the myth that it must be perfect the first time around! Listen! Even with this book! It is so likely that you will find a typographical error! Because when it comes to getting the word and message out there, done is better than perfect. And from done, anything can be redone. You will need and want the feedback of the market to create quality content that people will buy up. The market will tell you what it wants, and you can meet the markets needs with your own unique spin.

So, take on practicing doing and moving more than thinking, wishing, and hoping. No more standing in the mirror and reciting your money mantras. You're motivated, we get it. We've covered first base. The only way to second is one foot in front of the other. Any more time you spend trying to get motivated is now moving into procrastination. It starts to become the "getting ready to get ready" syndrome. That syndrome will keep you shuffling papers to look busy and shuffling your feet in circles. For the rest of this book, detach from the motivation piece and join me in movement.

I will also refer to movement as action, or inspired action. It is the thing between you and your dreams becoming your reality. More than that, it is the thing between you and your momentum. It is the bridge between where you are now and where you want to be. Movement proves to God or whoever you believe in that you are willing to have what you ask for. This is some secret sauce of The Cycle of Mastery because you don't get one without the others.

You are displaying to that higher power that you believe you deserve what you want. It is exercising your faith in your vision without sight about how you will get there. It is vision through the fog. Walking blind while your motivation pulls you is often required for you to get where you're going.

The next quarter of this book dissects movement so that you can get started chasing your dreams. Sometimes, it starts as a crawl. Then, you begin to wobble. Then a walk turns into a jog and finally, a sprint. By the time we're done with this book, you will be sprinting at a 100 miles per hour towards a life you say that you want!

Chapter 16

Two Types of People

In the second part of this book, I described the people who resist change, growth, and evolution. I wrote about them first because I am moving you through The Cycle of Mastery one step at a time. To notice that you resist change and avoid it can be the most powerful awareness. We had to start by pointing out "the resister" in us. Recognizing the part of us that avoids was necessary to generate some motivation. That motivation gets us to spring into action. Please don't spend any time being righteous about it. We all have a part of us that avoids discomfort and it is normal.

We avoid situations without realizing it. The constant avoidance behavior kills our motivation. When we understand this self-sabotaging pattern, we can shift away from this behavior. We have the power within to choose not to do that to ourselves. You can choose to stop your limiting beliefs. You can work out your fears and insecurities. You will feel the motivation to take massive strides in your life!

So now I'm speaking to the other half of the world. I am speaking to the other half of *you*. We all have these two halves and we all embody one of these identities with more prominence. Those of you who can sense change, honor it, and move right into it tend to speed up faster and go further than most. You'll step into and move right through the transition phase.

You are the kind who can sense change and jump into it. Like the seasonal migration of aquatic and terrestrial animals, you change. It is such a natural law of the universe to change, grow, and evolve. Thus, you can sense your natural-instinct to know that now is the time to grow through change.

That doesn't always mean that growth doesn't come with its own set of challenges and adversity. Yet, your willingness to go through it will make the journey less adverse. There seems to be less steep terrain along that path when you are willing to walk in the direction of your fullest life. Somehow, the willing experience less thick and thorny brush along the path of growth. The Sun and the Moon will light the way.

So, for those of you who can sense when it's time to change and start moving into it, I want to acknowledge you. I honor your pluck and bravery for taking charge of your life. It is so great to explain the two sides of us, or two types of people in the world. Many of you had to start by not resisting and avoiding. You're in a new head space of accepting change.

Choosing to move right into your transformation takes you to new levels. Intimate familiarity with change is the fuel for the massive momentum engine. To create massive momentum, you must have a willingness to change.

There's nothing wrong with change. There's nothing right about it either. It is a fact of life and a law of the universe. The only thing that *is* consistent in the universe is change and evolution. The more okay with this you become the more flow you will find and the more momentum you will create.

You must become okay with change. It took me stepping into movement that raised the needle of success for me. One major step of trust generated speaking gigs and radio shows. I will share that step here in a few chapters. Stepping into action had my life looking different than when I hoped and prayed for my big brakes.

So, without further ado, you must choose which of these 2 people you are going to be. It does not matter how you have been your entire life up until this point. You must choose now from the brand-new opportunity that this moment in time is.

If you find yourself still stuck and resisting change, allow my journey to be evidence. Allow my evolution to be evidence. You are in your process and on your journey. I invite you to write your own timeline of your life and look over your own evolution. You don't have to even be super detailed or in depth about it. Write out a bit of description of the 5 to 10 different phases of your life:

- Childhood
- Adolescence
- Middle school
- High school
- College
- First job
- First relationship
- Many relationships
- Traveling
- Divorce/Big break ups
- Sickness/Health/Illness
- Riches/Wealth/Poverty

These are a few examples of the different phases of your life. People tell stories of being bankrupt one year and a millionaire CEO the next. Your life comes in so many phases and stages. If you get stuck, you will not evolve. It is a prolonging of the destiny awaiting you. It is a disservice to those waiting for you to be a gift and be a light for them.

You are a light of God. God created you in His likeness. Endowed with divine gifts, you have the responsibility to develop and deliver them. Again, I invite you to step into your journey. You can transform into the most powerful version of yourself.

Do not quit because it gets scary or uncomfortable. Lean into the newness. Lean into the unknown. Allow yourself to discover something you've never known. You will experience a life with increased opportunity.

The unknown is only scary because it's unknown. It's like walking into a dark room. You don't fear walking into a light room because you can see everything. Everything is in plain sight for you to process. Turn the potential threats into gifts and blessings. Look for the opportunities in setbacks. Take courage when it is time to make a change. Pretend that you can see and soon you will. Use your own night vision to move you through what scares you. Walk towards your fullest future.

The perceived threat of moving through the unknown in life is temporary. The growth pains are temporary. The benefits of growth are immeasurable and leave a lasting impact on the quality of your life. The risk is worth the reward.

So, it is your time to choose to give up all resistance and step into the current of movement. That current will carry you with momentum. Your fullest life awaits.

Chapter 17
Doing Causes Movement

No matter how much experience I had as a teacher, I noticed that a lot of students came to class not prepared. It was most common at the beginning of semesters and with students new to my instruction. Student's lack of preparedness would cost us time in class. Students make extra trips to lockers for backpacks. This is disruptive in any classroom. In music instruction, this meant moving instruments and chairs and more. This needless process created many layers of frustration. From time to time their unreadiness challenged me on the many levels. Besides forgetting their supplies, they would test me by telling me that I did not show them how to play the song. Other times, they would forget the books and sheets. One of the best excuses that I ever heard was that I did not teach them correctly. That was the one that got me hot under the collar.

At first, I would explain that because I am an instructor, I need to come prepared to class every week. I explained that as my students, I expected them to come prepared to class as well. This seemed to be falling on deaf ears, so I decided to turn my talk into action. They thought teaching was easy, so I would have them instruct the class for about 10 minutes. From time to time, I would have a student take the baton and instruct their classmates on a warm up exercise or a song. I would have them teach and ask questions of their classmates.

As expected, this was challenging for the kids. They would overwhelm. Frustration increased due to lack of classmate preparedness and enthusiasm. The students had their eyes opened to the challenges of teaching. By doing this, my kids would understand more of what it takes to be up front leading the ranks.

The ones I picked to teach excelled afterwards. This kind of became a new thing. They would beg me from time to time to have someone teach while I observed. It was their smart way of telling me to shut up for least 10 minutes. I never did mind taking a seat to watch some of my student's brilliance and leadership shine.

There were weeks when I would announce to the students who was going to teach the class for next week. Yet, there were other weeks where I would stop in the middle of class and sit down. A selected student would teach until I told them to stop. This took about a good month to show results. I saw students starting to practice more. I saw students start to ask more questions. They became more engaged in the class. It was working.

Pop quizzes were something that I grew up with to keep us prepared for anything in class. This became my student's pop quiz. I would put them in front of the class without notice. Now they had come to understand that they had to be even more prepared. I must say, it was a pretty entertaining watching them in the beginning.

Once they got a taste of what it was like to be in front of the class, I took a step further. The student that I chose as temporary instructor had to grade their classmate's songs. This didn't impact their grades, just their experience and maturity. They did not like that at first because it was a song they did not learn. This was a fresh, new challenge that I could tell was growing them.

I used this exercise to further teach them how to read music and I would encourage them as they graded. I would ask them to decide if the song was played correctly or not. This took a little bit more time. Yet, I found it very rewarding watching them get better. They not only played music, but their reading and grading music improved.

As a teacher, it made me so proud to watch them pick it up and evolve as musicians and people. I saw that these kids didn't just learn to come to class prepared. They came to understand what it was like to be engaged in their learning. Many of them have displayed that this life's lesson also got them prepared as they became young adults.

This ever so important life lesson translates into your life in this very moment. Doing causes moving! You can read this book 15 times over. You can put it down after many chapters and begin applying the lessons to your life and causing some of them to last. You can stand up at the podium and take the baton in your life and begin orchestrating the many factors at play.

It's worth repeating. You can sign up for all the programs without coming to your life prepared. Any instructor will become that teacher that you couldn't stand. The program will become another one that does not work for you. You will play the victim card. You will become cranky and resentful. You will feel broken as if there is something wrong with you. You keep insisting that you don't have to show up to your life as the leader and creator of it. You are not willing to be the one instructing the instrumentals creating the song of your life.

Millions of people go through an education system. These educated people use about 10-

15% of what they learned. Then, they will sign up for coaches and courses to attempt to fix the broken or missing pieces in their life. They tell themselves, "If I was 'this way' or knew 'this thing' then I could succeed!" Well, as your coach I am here to call BS on that mentality.

You can keep trying to fix what you think is wrong with you or you can get into action around your dreams. Doing causes moving. Getting up out of your seat and becoming the leader that you are will teach you the lessons that you need to learn. Doing will take your life further.

So, stop sitting around and start getting responsible for the quality of your life. It's time to start moving. You can either keep reading and take it as instruction or you can stop right here. Start journaling and applying the lessons in this book to your life. Take a moment to answer the following questions:

- What is it that I want? Be as detailed as possible.
- On a scale of 1 to 10, how committed am I to having it?
- If not a 10, what's in the gap between where I am and where I want to be?
- What is there for me to learn to become level 10 ready to take on my life?
- What support do I need?
- What's missing for me?

- If I had what seems to be missing, what would make the difference in my progress, success, and results?
- What are the best ways that I like to be supported?

Chapter 18

Getting on the Plane

Something profound happened that changed the direction and trajectory of my life. In 2016, I got on a plane for the first time in 15 years. It represented a step past the threshold of being stuck. That movement caused the momentum that has created this book for you.

I'd like to break down the concept of "getting on the plane of life."

Consider you're going on a trip. There are a lot of steps involved. There is the packing and getting to the airport. You have checking in and getting through security. You must include getting to the gate, on the plane, and in the air. You are about halfway there.

Use the imagery of the stops to create motivation, movement, and momentum in your life. It is a perfect representation of The Cycle of Mastery. I would like to break it down further and encourage you fit this into an example that means the most to you. Maybe it translates to going to your favorite concert or skiing the slopes. Whatever works to get you buzzing with excitement to use The Cycle is to your advantage.

Most often, looking up a plane ticket happens in motivation. You get all excited because you have enough money. You have a travel buddy confirmed, or vacation days available. The circumstances provide you enough inspiration to book your next trip.

Then, there is the process of packing and getting to the airport. These are all subtle movements in the direction of your trip. They're not the most exciting or fun part of the process. Mundane movements include logistics, planning, thoughts, lists, and considerations. Also, it requires some organizing. You need to organize a ride to the airport, travels mates, boarding passes, and more.

You finally end up at the airport and the movement is not over. It's time to check in. This is where the real transformation starts to occur. First, you drop off any baggage you have at check in. This already begins to lighten your load as you move forward toward your destination. To proceed, there is identity check after identity check. Think about this in direct correlation with your growth as an entrepreneur. You are being checked by the "Success Security" entry after entry. You must always show your credentials. You confirm your belonging. You must prove that you have a seat on the plane to get anywhere near it. The travel process requires motivation and consistent action to arrive at your destination.

The process of going through security can be either tougher or easier at different times of life. All the while these challenges stretch and teach you the rules of travel and the rules of life. To learn how to get through "Success Security" will get you through growth periods.

Too many people get an attitude about going through security. When you realize that there's nothing bad happening *to* you, you can relax. You can glide through the process without any feelings about it. Some people sense change and jump right into the current. Lack of resistance makes moving through a security check a painless process. Getting through security is part of the process. By accepting that fact, you can begin to accept that to get where you're going you must go through it.

This means stripping down and removing anything that will trip the metal detector. You can walk through the body scanner as yourself. Know that you'll make it through to the other side without a hitch. Once you're able to do that, you can always put your baggage back on if you wish.

Your baggage is your choice. Once you make it through a checkpoint in life, you will realize a new level of capability. You have access to new destinations that you didn't a moment before. Once you do clear your way, you're able to grab what you need and then continue your journey. Experienced travelers begin to better understand all the nuances of traveling. They pack lighter and glide right through security.

From this point, the journey gains traction and becomes more fun. After smooth sailing past security, you are home free to your flight! You may have time to grab a coffee, a beer, or get a bite to eat. You may be rushing to your destination and have no time to waste. Either way, the journey looks different for everybody. It can even look different flight to flight for yourself.

Finally, you end up at the gate! You've made it to the plane and now it's time for take-off! This *still* requires a whole new section of the process! You are *still* not near your destination! There are *still* hours and miles between where you are now to where you want to be! YIKES! Anyone tired of transformation yet? Is traveling this worth it? Can you tell why so many don't do as much as they would like?

Like the toughest, most high paying jobs, there is a natural filtration system I like to refer to as "tough." Traveling this much must become a priority. It is time, money, and energy consuming. Because of that, many people do not choose it as often as they say they would like. Many people to do not choose change, because they can see the time, money, and energy it would cost them.

Instead, they choose comfort or security. The freedom of flying or owning your business looks more burdensome in the eyes of many and they avoid it. Excuses get made about why they cannot do what they want in life. Many don't see how it is a direct result of the way they avoid and resist changing old thought patterns. They do not make their dreams a priority. Over time, this attitude will cost so many people their light-heartedness. They forget what it's like to dream and soar.

Speaking of soaring, let's get back to your flight. It is time to board. Yet there is another "Success Security" check point. In life, you will always be tested and if I have to be the one for you right now, I am happy to be that test. STOP expecting life to get "easier!" At all the different levels of life, those that depend on you will expect you to live up to a new standard of living. There are endless security check points in life. Check points include birthdays, tax season, new jobs, new homes, relationships, and more. I implore you not to live the same year over again many times in succession, and then call it a life. I don't even believe that you would have made it this far in the book without commitment. You want a full life.

Many of the people you love and care about live a resistant life. They give up traveling to foreign lands. Please don't stop your own travel. Do not give anything up because your loved ones may not get your priorities. Stay the course. Keep covering the uncharted territories of your heart and mind. You will be thankful that you took off every chance that you could. Take the risk. Take the trip. Start the biz. Follow your dreams with vigor!

So here you are! You have made to your seat on the plane! I don't know why more people don't shout and cheer more for this victory! Today the phenomenon of flight has become so common that we forget the actual feat of mankind that it is.

You can bet I wasn't exactly shouting and cheering on my first flight in 15 years. I was sweating and panting. I had nearly forgotten what it was like to board an enormous machine. The miracle of flight could alter my reality within a few hours. Despite some of my nerves, the gratitude that overcame me had me sitting in my seat in awe and with reverence. I felt overwhelmed by this huge life step I was taking into the current of transformation. I didn't exactly know what lie ahead but I knew that my life would never be the same and I was right.

So here we all are on this plane analogy of transformation, buckled in and picking up speed! We are jetting down the runway and this is when the people most afraid of change receive an alteration. It is in this moment that we must surrender the grip we have on control to the pilot. Higher Power, God, Universe or whatever you call it is taking the wheel on your life.

You did your part. You got the ticket, got to the airport and the plane. You've passed all the challenges and adversity. You have proven your commitment. It is time to sit back a bit, relax, and enjoy some free drinks.

This isn't a one-man job anymore. You can only get so far on your own. You cannot take off without support and structure. The pilot and his crew are on your team. The acceleration in the momentum phase of your life will be based on the movement phase of your life. If you are serious about going anywhere far and often in life, it will need a team.

So here we go, racing down the runway, catching speed. "Front wheels up, back wheels up, and we're off." We're catching air, taking flight, and soon to be soaring through the skies, on the way to your destination.

If you are impatient about the destination, keep in mind that you have connecting flights. Life makes you take off and land many times to get where you're going. I want to normalize this up and down feeling. Every flight is a new growth. Every security checkpoint is the time to strip down and sprint through. You don't get to have the life you want if you are not willing to create the movement. It takes movement to board the plane. Momentum comes from taking the flight to a destination.

I learned this lesson so well and so many times over since 2016. I've been on 7 flights since then and have learned new lessons each time around. I learned to create the kind of momentum you want in your life, you must be willing to make the movement. You must get on the plane. You must board. Drop your baggage and go. If it wasn't for finally getting on the plane, I wouldn't have created the momentum in my business. I will share that with you in the next part of this book.

So, do the damn thing. Get crystal clear on your priorities and act. Your life reflects your priorities. Your words mean nothing without results. Your motivation is a bunch of hot air or jet fuel fumes without movement. You cannot get anywhere without getting on the plane.

Chapter 19

There's Only One Direction from Death

Motivation without intentional movement can send you to far-off lands. You don't want a random destination. It's like getting in the car with no destination and driving around. That is what we call a joy ride. While joy rides are fun on a Sunday afternoon, they are not the same as getting to work on a Monday morning. Drives to work have a different energy to them. There is clarity, focus, and determination. You know where you are going, how you are getting there, and how long it will take.

Getting in the car and driving without a map and a plan can take you miles out of your way. Having the drive to reach your goals is the same as your drive to work. It is *your* drive to your life's "work." You can find your destination on the roadmap. Use the distances on the roadmap to calculate time of arrival. Use a roadmap when you are serious about what you are up to and what you are creating.

You must have some version of a plan to get you where you're going. You must be clear about your destination and set up a strategy to get there. In my coaching, I call it a Roadmap. It serves as a reference tool along your way. It is a support structure to keep you on track. Many call the Roadmap backwards planning.

Since we've been talking about motivation, you've gotten clearer about what it is you want. The movement section of this book is about how to get from where you are now to where you want to be. A roadmap will get you there. In this chapter we will set you up with measurable, realistic steps to take.

When creating a roadmap, there are few things to consider. We are going to break this down into a few sections. So, get out your journal and get serious about your plan. Take your time on this chapter to begin creating your future with purpose and intention. Using this chapter for everything it is worth will add grease to the gears of your Cycle of Mastery. Use the following guided prompts to sort out your thoughts. Put them on paper and put them in an order that serves your movement and momentum.

Where are you now?

- What story do you tell others about yourself?
- What story are you telling yourself?

95

- What role does your past play in your present?
- What role does your future play in your present?
- What determines your motivation?
- What determines your movement?
- What is your biggest struggle?
- What is your biggest contribution to the world?
- What are you most passionate about?
- What keeps you up at night?

Where are you going?

- How far you are going?
- What are your 'mountain peak' visions you have for your life?
- How far away do your realized dreams seem to be right now?
- What do you want most?
- If you got to say so, what would your best version of your fullest life look like?
- If you had that life, what would be the experience you would be having of life?
- Why is this experience of life so important to you?

How long until you get there?

- How fast do you want to achieve your dreams?

- What you're going to have to give up along the way?
- What you're willing to give up along the way?
- What are you not willing to give up along the way?
- What barriers seem to be between you and your fullest vision?
- What exist in the gap between where you are and where you want to be?
- What is weighing you down or holding you back?

Stepping into inspired action:

- List the 5 biggest milestones between you and your goal
- List 5 mini milestones underneath each of those big milestones
- Who do you know who could help you get closer to your goal?
- Who do you already have on your team and in your corner?
- What actions are you avoiding taking?
- What actions have you felt called to take?
- What is one action you could take right now to get one step closer to your dream?

Now that you have finished these questions, sit back and take it all in. Review your answers as the beginning stage of your road map. Look over your answers with the perspective of your life in its totality. Now answer the following questions:

- What have you discovered in this exercise?
- What experience of life have you been having?
- What experience of life do you want to be having?
- What 3 things need to shift to create fresh motivation, movement, and momentum?
- What limiting beliefs are present on your Roadmap?
- What opportunities are available on your Roadmap?
- Do you see something new on the paper?

This paper is a roadmap of your thoughts, beliefs, fears, frustrations, and challenges. Avenues that were once concealed from your view suddenly reveal themselves to you. Your next actions become obvious and exciting. New ideas will present themselves. Challenges you never considered show up. Your mind opens-up in new ways and brilliant ideas come to the surface.

Getting your ideas out of your head and onto paper is one of the most powerful exercises you can do. It sets you free in ways that you can only experience by doing it. So, do it. Write, write, write, and write some more.

I like to keep a journal of brilliant thoughts that I have so that I do not have to use any extra energy trying to remember. When I write them out, it creates new head space and more ideas come to mind! Sometimes it is a brand-new idea or the next phase of an old one! I have thought up books, radio show episodes, and more with this strategy.

What sort of ideas do you have stored up in that noggin of yours? You may begin by writing out one dream or you can go straight for the total vision of your life. You can use the Roadmap concept time and time again. To sort out your thoughts, back away from the problem or opportunity. Get a bird's eye view of what it is you're dealing with. This will create clarity, presence, and excitement! Doing this will exercise your creative problem-solving skills. This process will present amazing new ways to tackle your dreams and make the most of your life.

What I love about this exercise is that it can get you present to how great you have it, how skilled you are. You can see all the resources you have available, and all the positive relationships you have. Relationships that can serve your mission, vision, and direction. Getting the stuff in your head on a tangible and visible Roadmap you can sort it out and set yourself up for success.

Any maps purpose is to get you from point A to point B. That is exactly what we're doing. We are getting you from where you are now to where you want to be and bridging the gap between it. You'll hear me say it many times throughout this book; life doesn't have to be a miserable struggle. It doesn't have to be decades of hard work and back breaking labor. It can be fun. You can be creative. You can live a full, abundant life without overworking your way through it.

You can use the power of your mind to create the life you want with minimal effort. The more Roadmaps you create, the more avenues to success you can take. This can lead to a life full of what you have created from your thoughts and motivation! As you continue to master The Cycle of Mastery, refer to this chapter often to generate your future.

Part IV:

The Power of You

Chapter 20

Snowball Effect

Before we jump right in to the last part of this book, I want to acknowledge you for using your motivation. Your motivation created the movement that has gotten you to the momentum phase of this book! You have arrived. No more waiting, wishing, or hoping. You're here. Your toes are on a new cliff of possibility and the only thing left to do is jump! It's time to enjoy the ride.

Momentum is not something you can pay for. It's not something someone else can give you. It does not exist anywhere outside of you. It is square in the middle of your chest.

The generation of momentum multiplies momentum. It only catches speed following action. To get warmed up to the idea of momentum, let's look at a few examples. Being on this new cliff of possibility, you speed up when you jump and begin to fall. You fall faster by the second.

The "Snowball Effect" is one of the most tried and true examples of momentum. Make a snowball. Set it on the ground, and roll it to begin collecting more snow, and then the snowball will grow in size. You could make an entire snowman this way or a boulder of snow! Add a slight slope to the ground and you would have that thing catching speed!

Speaking of downhill speed, an avalanche gets triggered by one sudden movement! A shift of the earth, one powerful jolt, and one crack can send an entire mountainside of snow rushing down. The avalanche eats up everything in its path. This is momentum. Momentum is a force of nature started by a movement. A human and nature can trigger movement. Like the avalanche your sudden movement can trigger momentum.

You can use one of the many laws of nature to your advantage in relationships, business, health, and life. An object in motion stays in motion. I will remind you of that rule because I want to bring another layer to it; energy. In the movement section of this book it was about getting up and going after it again and again and again. Now, it is about the movement of energy that your movement creates!

I want you to get something powerful. You are a force of nature. You are a force to be reckoned with! You are powerful beyond measure and when you get that, you can use it to cause your dreams to show up in your reality. You can turn a thought into a conversation.

You can turn a conversation into business. You can turn business into a business transaction. You can turn business transactions into money! You can turn money into more money!

And here we are right back at The Cycle of Mastery! Your thoughts are your motivation. Action is the bridge from where you are to where you want to be. Momentum is the manifestation of your combined thoughts and efforts! It is a systematic and powerful equation for you to take advantage of to create a life you dream of.

I know this so well because I have learned it through decades of trial and error. I did things not aligned with the progress of my business and life. This cost me happiness, health, money, energy, and motivation.

I kept trying to get away with minimal effort for greatest success. Getting started and sticking to anything seemed like such a daunting task. There were times that my "stretch towards success" amounted to 2 or 3 sales calls. I would make enough money to look successful, but I didn't reap fulfilling results.

It was when I bottomed out in every area of my life that I decided to make a real change to my self-destructive patterns. When I had $300 suits in my closet and couldn't afford wheels on my car, I woke up. It stung my pride to have to borrow money from my parents when I felt like

I was handling my business. It was a reality check about how I was spending my money. I was clear that I wasn't using my success to create my momentum. My success stopped at my suits.

When I woke up to this and applied the lessons I was learning, I began making shifts all over my life. I switched up how I was spending my money. I began getting more conscious about what I was eating. I became more selective about who I was making business exchanges with. When I redirected my efforts, my life began to catch momentum in the direction I wanted it to be going.

In this last section of the book, I will explain how to use momentum to take your life in the direction you want it to go. I will share a few more missteps and huge strides that I took as I grew in my understanding of momentum. Now, I bring these lessons to you as you take on your greatest life.

Chapter 21

You Get Out What You Put In

It's true. There may be no stronger law. The law of attraction. You get out what you put in. Hate breeds hate. Love breeds love. Wanting creates more wanting. Doing generates more doing. Growth leads to more growth.

- Can you feel the momentum?
- How many times in your life have you proven this truth unwavering?
- How many phases of life can you see pattern this evident?
- How many times will God have to teach you the lesson before you learn it?
- When you accept this truth as law, will you choose love?

Consider humanity's thought leaders:

- Tony Robbins
- Bob Proctor
- Robert Kiyosaki
- Dan Clark

- Dale Carnegie
- John C. Maxwell
- Robert Greene

When they learned how to manifest wealth of mind, body, and soul, they chose to teach it. When we gain access to plenty, there is nothing left to do but share it. This truth brings this book from my mind to your fingertips.

Our super power is to apply our lessons to support our brothers and sisters along their soul's path. When we learn to do this, we win. I bring this book to you to share my story and support your journey as you create your greatest life. You are well on your way and picking up speed.

As we move forward, I will remind you of the universal truth. You get what you put in. The sooner you accept that, the quicker you will get to the most powerful version of you. You have super powers right now. Put them into the world and get the world back.

This lesson can be comparable to a retirement plan. You must be the one to make the investment and the company is the one to match it. When you take inspired action, you are making an investment in your life, business, and more.

It is after your example that God matches your efforts and throws the matching momentum your way. Inexplicable surprises come your way. Things just seem to work out. People come into your life to support and guide you. This creates a swirl of progress and a swirl of speed your way. This is momentum.

Momentum comes as a result of your actions that the universe can hear and respond to. Steady action around your dreams is a necessary and often overlooked step. Steady action generates momentum.

Momentum isn't something to do. Momentum is a *result of* the things you do. So, if you want the life you say you want and you aren't experiencing it yet, I invite you to go reread the movement chapter.

If you haven't generated some crazy action in your life yet, it's time. It is time to roll your sleeves up and put out what you want coming in. Momentum is a result of consistent movement. I will share it as persistence in the next chapter. Let's wrap up this chapter with some flexing your faith in this refreshed lesson. Announce these examples out loud and then journal some more of these examples that apply to you. Announce more accurate versions for yourself:

- Focus out, focus in
- Interest out, interest in
- Deals out, deals in
- Happy out, happy in
- Sharing out, sharing in
- Networking out, networking in

- Sale calls out, sale calls in
- Love out, love in
- Promises out, promises in
- Anything out, anything in

You are so capable of producing whatever you desire. What in your life and business have you been avoiding? What have you not done since you've begun reading this book? What "aha" moments have you had and applied?

Do you catch yourself wanting something different for your life? If so, you need to understand how you are responsible for the way your life is. This can be THE game changer. Get clear that the quality and direction of your life is your responsibility. To find out what you are putting out, get real with yourself and examine what is coming in. This will reveal the energy and effort you are applying to your goals and visions.

So now that you get how consistent this law of attraction is you can begin using it on purpose. You will blow your own mind with your power when your actions match your words and visions. Begin putting out what you want to come back to you.

Do the thing. Send the email. Make the call. Ask for the date or promotion. Start the project. Write the book. Sell the program. Buy the investment. Do the Damn Thing! Your life depends on it. The quality of your life depends on it.

Few stay consistent enough in their efforts to learn this lesson. Go further than anyone you know. Stay the course with what you are passionate about. Notice what you care and talk about most and do it more. Let your deepest powers take over and evolve. Pour your skills and gifts into the world more and more. You will not only make the world a better place, you will create a thriving life from it.

It is your persistence that gets paid. It is your commitment to your highest good. When you shine, you brighten the world. When you are a light of hope, you have a gravitational pull. Light out, light in. Love out, love in. Abundance out, abundance in. Let your light shine.

Chapter 22
Power of Persistence

I'm sure you've heard it and if not, allow me to be the first to tell you, the only way you can fail anything is to quit. So, cliché and yet, it is so true and powerful.

Now let's sort this concept out completely. I'm a believer in healthy quitting. Quitting the things that no longer serve you. Quitting relationships that no longer serve you. Quitting anything that doesn't serve your greater purpose and your biggest goals. When you are saying "Yes" to please others or doing what you think you *have* to do, is keeping you stuck in mediocrity. Quitting things that slow you down or negate your progress are important to leave behind.

What I'm going to encourage you to persist with is your fullest self and your fullest life. To live your fullest mission here on Earth, you must become laser focused on your development.

You must persist at all costs to truly receive the breakthrough of momentum.

The momentum you pray for comes from persistence of movement. Become willing to always step forward no matter what. Become willing to leave things behind. You won't be taking everything from your past into your future. Become willing to take the next right step, the next inspired action, the next move. This consistent movement will build and grow into that Snowball Effect.

This hunger for success exceeds all fears and insecurities. Within the confines of good ethics and the law, you do what it takes to succeed no matter what. Persisting looks like picking up the phone and making a "scary" call. It looks like making a bold request, accepting an offer, or taking in what seems like a million "No's for the one Yes." Persisting shows up! The most important part to know is that it will take you past every single edge of your comfort zone.

Continue to take the next right step. It doesn't always have to be at a 100 miles per hour. Persisting may just look like sending one more email or making one more phone call. I encourage you to do at least one more hard thing for your business each day. It is okay and very normal to fall into times where staying optimistic and persistent is a challenge.

At different phases of entrepreneurship, your momentum feels like a crawl or a sprint. No matter what it feels like, keep going. Do not stop. Do not give up on your greatest self and your fullest life. There is a difference between taking a rest and quitting. Learn the difference and never stop.

I can promise you there is going to be days you will wonder why the hell you started and where the hell you're going. What I'm here to tell you is to persist in those times. The time that you want to quit the most is *the most vital* time to buck up and go further! Those are the times where you will let God know that you're not kidding around. You are not to be turned away. You are not to be discouraged or scared off by a challenge. You are clear about what you're up to and even in the toughest of times, you are willing to take one more swing.

Persisting is pursuing your greatest calling without quitting. You will get tired. You will doubt your abilities and sanity. I promise. I know. I have been there so many times and still go there in every new growth period. You must persist far past all the negative chatter going on inside your head. Persisting will get you exactly where you're going and take you to the highest mountain peaks.

You really cannot even comprehend how high you can go when you simply do not quit. It is unlikely your imagination is even aware of all that is truly possible. I am confident none of us know what God has in store for us. There is only one way to find out. We must become willing to keep moving into our calling.

With open hearts, eyes, and ears, we are called into each next direction. Before we know it, opportunities show up left and right. Delivered into situations that present the next step to take, we must operate in full trust. In self-mastery and entrepreneurship, this takes a lot of blind trust. Become comfortable getting uncomfortable. Practice using the power of your mind's eye, your vision, much more than your actual sight.

To achieve the biggest goals with the biggest impact, you must be able to envision your dreams. Tapping into the power of your mind is what will get you past all the barriers to success. Faith in the help from the good God Himself will keep you marching in the direction of your goals.

The only way to fail at that is to quit. Do not quit.

Chapter 23

Rest, Relax, and Repeat

There's something interesting about motivation, movement, and momentum. They are often so exhilarating and so rewarding that we forget to slow down at times. We either get carried away by the momentum or carried away by our vision. We become hyper focused on how we can get "there" and rev up the pace from 100 miles per hour into complete over drive.

While I encourage commitment and persistence, I also promote self-awareness, rest, and recuperation. Shifting from full speed to overdrive can cause break down. It is important to keep a healthy pace of growth that includes rest for your body and mind. Often when entrepreneurs take off, they hit their heads on a ceiling of self-care. If your personal health game is not on point and develops with you, you will max out from fatigue.

You have a responsibility to maintain the quality of your life in every aspect. Business is just one aspect. You must foster your relationships. It is vital to practice spirituality of some form. You must care for the body you have been given. It is the practice of self-care that separates the good from the great. Integrity in every area of your life is what elevates you to where you dream about being.

From the standpoint of motivation, self- care exists inside of an abundance mindset. In the abundance mindset, you trust that you have unlimited resources. You can choose whatever you want and go for it. From this mindset, you give yourself permission. You don't have to create anything. You just allow it into your life. The momentum section of this book encourages you to trust and lean into your abundance. Momentum is a force of nature, not a force of you.

The self-sabotage that we struggle with lives inside of a scarcity mindset. Complaints about not enough time, money, energy, and more, there is never enough of anything. You never feel ready to act. You are always waiting for enough and that will never seem to be the case. When we have this complaint, we think that we have a valid reason to stay stuck and it looks like it's not our faults. We can blame and shame forces outside of us for our misfortune.

The Cycle of Mastery is really the Mastery of Self. We must become in tune with our mind, body, and soul to keep making our next best steps. Awareness of the power of choice allows us to use motivation, movement, and momentum. In cases where we are super disconnected, our dreams and success seem unreachable.

The worst times in my business were the worst times in my full-scale well-being. My wellness suffered, and the suffering caused a spiraling downward. Spiraling health harmed every area of my life. From relationships to income, I felt like I was losing my grip on my power, direction, and my momentum. I would ignore my heath and choose self-sabotaging patterns that stunted my growth.

I would over eat, kick back, and drink up during the good blips in my business. I would land one or two new clients with minimal effort and feel that rush of relief from a hefty paycheck or two. I would shop for a new suit with my commission checks before paying the bills. I would make sure that I purchased the newest phone, but I couldn't afford wheels on my car. This lifestyle was not a sustainable one and I had to learn it over and over for the lesson to stick.

You may have noticed that there are some habits and patterns that you cannot keep as you grow. You will drop many situations and relationships as you elevate your way. The façade will fade because it won't fit in your new

117

phases. Heavy partying and sleep deprivation will become a thing of the past. They will lose their appeal.

One of those early entrepreneur appeals has always been "work hard, play hard," right? We have heard it our whole lives. I always ended up playing harder than I worked and it cost me every time. Undoubtedly, this pattern caused a dip in my business and progress. I was buying things that I couldn't afford. I was skipping out on working for myself with consistency. My self-development game suffered. Playing the part by looking the part or taking shortcuts to success wasn't working. I couldn't even maintain the facade anymore. I was becoming exhausted by this quicksand type of feeling. Money was flying out of my hands faster than it was coming in and after a few years of this, it hit me like a ton of bricks. "What do I have to show for all my efforts?" I needed a break and I could feel it in every bone in my body. This is when I learned the difference between "play hard" and rest.

At one point in my hustle and grind pattern, I discovered I had a fractured bone in my hand. I had no idea when and how I had broken it. It had been bothersome for a while, but I kept ignoring it to persist. "I don't have time for this!" I would criticize my own hand. Typing became a challenge. Daily routines were taking longer. Shaking hands caused me to see stars from the sharp pain and became an excruciating task. You already know that I can't be having that! I've got way too many hands to shake to be out of commission. It finally started throbbing enough that I had to pay attention to it. So, to the doctor I went. Proper stabilization and rest were the only option. Stop what you are doing, clear your schedule, and get back into your body.

When we refuse to slow down and care for our bodies, very likely that God will strike us down. We *must* pay attention to messages sent. This is exactly what happened with my hand and I had to look up and admit to the big man, "Okay, I got it. I will slow down and reset." This slowing down allowed me to finish my next book with a clear mind. It gave me a fresh take on many of my projects. This also created a lot of clarity in the direction that I was taking my business. Rest generates head space. You must stop or slow down.

Sometimes, when we are hustling at the speed of light, we get so locked up in our head that we forget that we have a body. I have caught myself many times wishing that I didn't need sleep so that I could keep going. I wished I didn't have to work out so that I could use those hours on my business growth and development. I became so hungry to succeed that I didn't want to slow down to cook or eat. We are so sure that the only way to succeed is by going without. We wish away our need to take care of our needs. If that worked, it would have worked by now. You wouldn't be reading self-development books about how to break through. If that approach to life worked, you would already be gliding on your successes. You would already be flowing in The Cycle of Mastery. Balancing your needs with the demands of life is essential to your unlimited success.

The most common fear that comes up when I teach this is, "but Shannon, if I stop or slow down, I will lose momentum! I can't! I can't afford it! I do not want to lose the little momentum that I *do* have! If I stop, I will lose everything!"

Can you hear the scarcity mindset at play? I totally get it because I have been there. I can speak to it because I have lived it too. I am telling you that you must become willing to rest and refuel in your ventures. You must learn the difference between quitting and taking a breather. Understanding rejuvenation is a part of your forward motion. Forward motion will break you through to your next level of success.

I encourage persistent passion, but I am here to tell you that life is not meant to be a constant struggle. You don't have to work your fingers to the bone or wear yourself down to prove you are working hard at your success. When you learn to rest appropriately, you learn the value of it. Like most everything in life, you only learn this lesson by doing it. No one can learn the lesson of relaxation for you. You can see *everybody* in the world relaxing. They can attempt to tell you and teach you how to relax. I am telling you to relax right now and yet, you may not learn to. Proper relaxation, rest, and rejuvenation needs to be a part of your routine. It cannot be taught. It must just be done.

People learn to relax when everything else gets taken away. People accept relaxing after they exhaust every single resource that they can. It is much like a tired toddler who will scream and mess himself for attention until he tires out and gives up. He runs out of steam to struggle and just let's go to breathe again. Soon, the tears dry and he's lying flat on his back with a bottle in his mouth relaxed.

I have thrown my adult temper tantrums when I was resisting my natural growth periods. My resistance didn't look like waving fists and stomping feet either. It was much more discreet in my adult years. My gut would be telling me that it was time to move forward and I would attempt to ignore it. I would avoid the urges I was getting to create bigger things. In my early

20's, I didn't understand that feeling, so I tried to suppress it instead of express it.

Only in looking back on it can I see that I did this with teaching music. I stayed longer than expected and let a few opportunities pass me by. I worked day and night jobs. I busied myself with busy work. I convinced myself that I was putting in the effort that would bring me the empire I dreamt of building. I would only dream of it from behind the podium or at my cubicle. Instead of going for it, I would spread my focus and motivation over many ventures. This diminished my motivation, killed my movement, and stopped much of my momentum.

I encourage rest and relaxation. Healthy rituals make you feel good. When you feel good, you produce good things. When you feel great, you produce great things! It is that simple. There is no way around proper self-care and maintenance. Time out to recuperate from hard work is essential to sustaining progress.

Entrepreneurs often struggle with a myth that if we lose momentum, we will lose progress. That is simply not true. You should strive for:

- Full weekday off
- Regular sleep
- Hydration
- Healthy eating habits
- Giving up vices and addictive behaviors

Also, part of rest and recovery includes mental health services and wellness check-ups. Your power cannot be easily depleted when cared for. These things are part of a sustainable lifestyle of a highly successful entrepreneur.

I hear people chasing their dreams say, "once I get there, then I can relax!" It could not be more backwards. You must incorporate relaxation into your current schedule to maintain the momentum. If you are not responsible for your self-care, it will catch up with you. You will feel like you are running on a treadmill going nowhere. There were phases in my life where I was just standing, and the treadmill wasn't even on! I used to even think that if a treadmill had a "go backwards" setting, that would be the direction I felt I was going.

Get serious about incorporating appropriate self-care into your regimen. If you do, you will enjoy the experience of chasing your dreams. If you don't, the passion for the work you love will fizzle. If you let this happen, you will quit or take a momentum murdering break. Are you there yet? Have you experienced this before?

I have no doubt at some point we all get there. We can shut off our humanity and chase with relentless fury. We would rather deny our natural human functions and needs to become robotic to achieve. When we are working from that mentality, we are also missing out of on the humanness of success. There is no fulfillment and joy. To deny one emotion is to deny them all. Become okay with your needs, emotions, and messages you receive from your body, mind, and soul.

One of the most backwards part of this equation is that the more self-care you have, the more success you have. The more you make yourself a priority, the more the universe makes you a priority. The more you chose you, God will understand that you respect the vessel that you've been given. You can deliver your gift longer and more fully. I implore you to honor the vessel and the gifts you've been given by restoring them often.

Take care of the hands that write, cook, and hold. Take care of the feet that carry you. Take care of the vocal cords, mouth, ears, and eyes that help your communication. Every organ in your body serves your purpose and mission. For those of you born with an ailment or a handicap, it was all part of your greater purpose. It all fits the puzzle. It all fits into the way that you will deliver your gift. Your spirit chose your vessel long before arriving. God placed you in exactly the perfect place, time, and purpose.

Trust it. Honor it. Love it. Take care of it. Restore it and continue to deliver your gift boldly, powerfully, and proudly. Do this by loving what you've got. Take care of the life you've been given, and it will take care of you.

Chapter 24
Resiliency

Resilience is your ability to bounce back. It is also known as rebounding. I like to use the classic term "The Comeback" as well! I like to call it anything that represents you getting back up off your butt when you've been knocked down by life.

It happens to us all. I'm sure you understand. We are always extra tough on ourselves when we take a few steps back in our progression towards our goals. You should accept the fact that you're not alone in this occurrence. Setbacks happen in life. You must be able to give up any struggle story that you have about how tough it is. We got it. It's tough. I have been in that frustration far too many times. We are growing together in this process. It doesn't have to be an absolute miserable struggle to chase your dreams.

The "get back up" attitude is the one that keeps you showing up to your entrepreneurial climb. Without resiliency, your passion and persistence will dwindle quickly. Resiliency looks like resting when you need a breather. It is allowing you to forgive any mistakes made. You can let go of missteps, investments that didn't payout, commitments that fell through, and more. Forgiving others if you feel betrayed or burned will help you feel freer to bounce back. Forgiveness will make your burden light after disappointment.

It is when you can begin to relate to a setback as a redirection that you can use it to your advantage. When you can accept that everything works or "doesn't work" for your best interest, you can shift your focus. You can shift your focus from the upset to the next come up. Remembering this and using it often will help you climb higher each leg of the journey.

We do not even realize that it is our triggered childhood memories that hold us back as adults. It is the "lessons" we learned as youngsters that stop us from taking chances. Chances occur as risks. When we "failed" or shamed as children, we put together a sort of cause and effect tracking system. "If I say the wrong answer, they will laugh at me." "When I don't get picked, they don't like me." "If I fail, I am a loser." Our adolescent minds log those hurtful memories in as red flags to look out for and avoid. Because of this, we adapt and stop putting ourselves out there. We stop trying new things and taking chances that can transform the quality of our life.

Because of insecurities from our childhood, we do not choose to be resilient. You may have been told that you we're not good enough. You may have been talked down to. It could have been that you were told that your ideas were stupid, you were stupid, or that you were worthless. Without our awareness as youngsters, we take on what we are told by others as beliefs about ourselves. We limit our possibility and persistence with those negative thoughts. Because of that, we never really "go for it" when something seems challenging. We don't believe we can achieve it.

In any sense, whatever your negative self-image, I invite you to get real about it. I want you to know that what happened in your past is not happening to you right now in your present. The people and events of the past are behind you. You are the one who keeps those memories, feelings, and belief systems alive. Those keep your self-sabotage pattern strong and suffocating. Teaching you about resilience is vital to momentum. You cannot have one without the other.

I want to provide you with a powerful tool to use as you go further past the limitations of your comfort zone. Any time that you have "failed" at something, know that it was simply an insufficient effort to create.

For example, if you want to make a million dollars a year and you make one sales phone call a day. That is 365 sales phone calls. You sell products that cost $1000. At a 20% closing rate, you will close about 73 people that year. That will make you $73,000. This is clearly is an insufficient strategy at making your million. There is nothing wrong, right, good, or bad about you in this example but you failed to meet your goal.

This failure can lead to discouragement. You could see this failure as a reason to quit on the million-dollar goal. You could buy into your limiting belief system that you are not good enough and people don't like you. That it is hard to sell your product, the economy is tough, and so on. You could come up with a million excuses before you hush that negativity.

If you want to make a $1,000,000 in a year selling a $1,000 product, then you need to be successful on 1,000 sales phone calls. Even at a high 30% close rate, you would need to make around 3,500 sales calls that year. That is 9-10 calls a day. This is completely manageable and totally different than the one a day strategy.

If you begin to get real about the statistics required to succeed, your resiliency will come to the table. With clarity that the effort made are insufficient, you can always recalibrate. You can offer up the hard work commensurate with your ideals of success. It's not as emotional as you believe it to be. Have you considered what it would take to reach your goals? Do you know your real goals? Let's take a more realistic look:

- How much do you want to be making?
- Do you know the real cost of the life that you dream of?
- Do you have many streams of income?
- Do you have any different priced items?
- Have you considered how many of your products or services you would need to sell to make as much as you dream of making?
- What do you even want for your life and your business?
- What is your definition of success?

Getting back up every time you fail will be based on how clear you are about your vision and your roadmap. The big vision questions and detailed strategy are vital to the execution of a plan. Reference your roadmap often. Stay clear about what you're up to, where you're going, and how you're getting there. Also include your plan to get back up when you get knocked down.

Resilience is also known as grit. It is your ability to persist when all signs point to "No." Your willingness to persist will take you to levels of success that others only wish and hope for.

With Cycle of Mastery skills, you will have the power to persist. You persist even in the face of no agreement from your family, your friends, or your business partners. When others doubt and you feel fear, you will not stop. When insecurities of childhood memory try to block success, you will be able to bulldoze them.

Your ability to dream so big it would feel uncomfortable to let people with small minds know how big you dream. They would not be able to understand why you "chose to keep putting yourself through this." Although they may love you, they may not understand how or why you're able to get back up every single time you take a hit.

With vivid clarity, commitment, and persistence that your resiliency will shine through. You sense yourself as completely unstoppable, unshakable, and unbreakable. Your resiliency will be a natural by-product of your faith in your vision. So, as you begin to develop your grit, create a roadmap so clear that nothing can get in the way. No one can stop you. Failures will not prevent you from persisting towards your purpose and passion. This will be a tell that you have mastered yourself. You can operate with full motivation, movement, and momentum.

Chapter 25

100 Miles in the Wrong Direction

You can generate momentum in the opposite direction of your focused destination. We as entrepreneurs are naturally "Yes" people. We love to please and win. It is always so tempting to take on new projects and roles because we can. This is an example of how our leadership mentality can lead us into too many commitments. This autopilot type of "Yes" can have us feeling overextended and ineffective everywhere. It leads to burnout and loss of willingness to pursue our passions.

If you are not responsible for what you want, you can end up in the trenches. Work in the trenches will teach you some of the hardest learned lessons. You will always learn a lesson. But without awareness, many entrepreneurs end up getting an inaccurate idea of entrepreneurism. That is why so many businesses fail in the first few months or years of starting up. The lack of business savvy ends up outweighing the passion or idea.

This pattern causes new entrepreneurs to doubt themselves. They doubt their idea, and the demand for what they are supplying. A negative relationship of being a business owner is born and the unraveling begins. Debts, bad transactions, unequal exchanges, and more come from situations at this level. It becomes more evidence for the struggling entrepreneur that they weren't cut out for this work.

The excuses start rolling in and the passion starts fading. This to me is one of the saddest parts of the growth period. There are so many casualties who never make it further than a few months or years. They never reach their fullest potential. With a bit of support and guidance, a new business owner's story doesn't have to end in defeat or despair. So many needless defeats make me sad.

Going 100 miles in the wrong direction is not all bad. In fact, it is quite predictable for those of us who launch businesses from ideas or sparks of passion. Many people don't have a business degree starting out. There are more people starting businesses on a hope and a prayer rather than on a business degree. No part of your life is wasted. No phase of the journey is pointless or squandered, I promise. These lessons are essential for growth. Of course, they would be learned in the first few years of your business.

It is up to you to read this and let it be your lesson to keep going through the growth periods. If serious about success, you will hear me when I tell you to get a business coach. Of course, continue to read books like this and join courses. Remember, you are not a failure, your attempts at success were insufficient. One sale-call a day isn't going to get you there. Your first book or social media post may not be your breakthrough moment. Not every video or episode you publish goes viral. One marvelous brave move isn't going to break down the barrier to success. Your success mindset will build your business, dream, and empire. Your success is just a matter of time if you choose so. Success is always available to you. You can always make your way around a learning curve faster if you are more aware, present, and observant.

That is precisely why The Cycle of Mastery starts with motivation and then movement. If you move without clarity, you may end up lost, frustrated, and confused. Often, our pride gets us fixated on a certain outcome that we focus on. We become consumed by winning a battle over a war. For example, we stay at a job we hate for too long. We can't seem to break off a relationship that no longer makes us better. We stay in a living environment that doesn't bring us joy. We want to avoid the feeling of failure. So, we refuse to quit or walk away from something that is holding us back or keeping us small. These examples keep us stuck. They often carry us further away from our mind's mission, out heart's desires and our soul's purpose. It is the lack of clarity and commitment that can carry us off 100 miles in the wrong direction.

Most entrepreneurs want to make great money while making a great difference in the world. If we let everything distract, it is likely that achieving our goal will take 5 times longer. The importance of the goal warrants unwavering focus. When you get motivated, you tend to chase any opportunity that presents itself. You will say "Yes" to anything that seems exciting. Yet, chasing each opportunity, you may find yourself lost.

Everyone will take what they can from you. This isn't always from a hurtful, vindictive, or spiteful place. If you are a "Yes" man or woman to everyone then that is exactly how they will treat you. You teach people how to treat you. They act in accordance to how you treat you. Learn this lesson and apply it every single day if you want your dreams to become your reality. If you do not value your dreams, neither will the people you surround yourself with.

It is in our human nature to survive. It is in our nature to use people and things to serve our goals. When someone offers you an opportunity, you must get out your own Roadmap. You must see if it aligns with the direction that you're taking your entire life. If it's not, it becomes a clear "No." If the opportunity can take you further, you can consider the pros and cons of working with someone. You can take the job and hire a coach. If it's completely aligned with your business, take it on full force, jump in with 2 feet, and never look back.

Intentional movement takes you in the direction you want to go. If you don't know what you want, you'll be much like a leaf in the wind. The wisp of the air will take you with it and you may end up in an unrecognizable land. Heed my warning, this is how you end up 100 miles in the wrong direction. You will have to navigate your way back to your own trail. The back tracking will leave you tired, pissed off, and discouraged. Experiences of life, relationships, and business *do not* have to go this way.

Continue to look back at and shape your Roadmap with as much detail as you can. Add together the different components of your life and see how they lineup together. Look at what runs parallel, what crosses over, and what's going in opposite directions. Clarity about these factors will help you decide where your priorities lie. Stay the course and you won't have to leave the trail too far in any direction.

Chapter 26
Conclusion

As we begin to wrap up our time together, I want to emphasize The Cycle of Mastery. It has come up hundreds of times in this book whether I have said it directly or have spoken about it conceptually. The Cycle of Mastery is this book. Your life and your success rely on it. Mastering yourself generates your movement mastery.

I share this so strongly and without discretion. I truly want to make a lasting difference in the trajectory and speed of your life. I have spent this book empowering your momentum towards where you envision it going. I am committed that you have the life you want. I am committed in serving you along your journey in getting there.

I have served you from my experience and own mastery. I have had hundreds of mentors and coaches along the way. I've tried every which way to succeed. Some ways have worked, and some ways have not. I have packaged these lessons and bring them to you in this book.

It has been an honor to contribute to you and your process. My hope for you is that you take these lessons and strategies and apply them to every area of life. Master yourself and you will master every aspect of life. Life will become simple. You can learn to enjoy the journey and thrive. When you are free instead of forced, success can flow into your life with fun, joy, and ease.

Most exciting of all, when you are the master of yourself, you become capable of assisting others. It is a level that I have reached, and it brings me such joy to turn around and serve. I love to coach and support others the way I have been supported and helped along the way. I have brought you decades of lessons to begin applying to your life so that the ripple effect may continue.

If you do not feel momentum in your life yet, it is okay. Go back to the chapters that may have not sunk in or clicked for you yet. You can read this book 10 times over and discover something new each time. You will be at a new place in your life and business each time. You cannot learn it all at once. The growth will always come in phases and stages and this has been a wonderful phase.

Beyond this book, join me along my journey. I have courses and one-on-one coaching. Also, I speak across the nation and on the airwaves.

Conclusion

Our journey doesn't end here. It starts here. I am here for you. I am here for your life and I want you to win as much as you do.

Don't quit on your dreams. Don't let a few bumps in the road and lumps on the head stop you from realizing your vision. Chase your dream no matter what. I am with you and you are so capable of achieving your dreams and living a life you create.

Never forget that you are also sent here to do that for others. If you have an entrepreneurial mindset, you were placed on this Earth to do exactly that. Now, go forth, live your dreams, and support others in doing the same. You will make this world a better place by mastering yourself. You will generate the motivation, movement, and momentum to change the world. Now, it is your turn.

Made in the
USA
Monee, IL